THE ANGUS LECTURESHIP.

VI.

SIDE-LIGHTS ON NEW TESTAMENT RESEARCH.

1908.

Side-Lights

ON

New Testament Research.

SEVEN LECTURES

DELIVERED IN 1908, AT REGENT'S PARK COLLEGE,
LONDON.

BY

J. RENDEL HARRIS,

M.A., D.LITT., &c.,

Director of Studies at the Woodbrooke Settlement, Selly Oak,
Near Birmingham.

WIPF & STOCK · Eugene, Oregon

Wipf and Stock Publishers
199 W 8th Ave, Suite 3
Eugene, OR 97401

Side-Lights on New Testament Research
Seven Lectures Delivered in 1908, at Regent Park's College, London
By Harris, J. Rendel
Softcover ISBN-13: 979-8-3852-0954-5
Hardcover ISBN-13: 979-8-3852-0955-2
eBook ISBN-13: 979-8-3852-0956-9
Publication date 12/7/2023
Previously published by The Kingsgate Press, 1909

This edition is a scanned facsimile of the original edition published in 1909.

PRELIMINARY NOTE.

THE ANGUS LECTURESHIP has its origin in a Fund raised as a testimonial to the Rev. Joseph Angus, M.A., D.D., as an expression of the sense entertained by the subscribers of his character and services as President of the Baptist Theological College, formerly situated at Stepney and now at Regent's Park, London. Dr. Angus having intimated his desire that the Fund should be devoted to the establishment of a permanent Lectureship in connection with the College, a Trust has been constituted for the purpose; its income to be "administered and applied by the College Committee for the establishment and maintenance of a Lectureship, to be called the 'Angus Lectureship,' in connection with the said College, for the delivery of periodic lectures on great questions connected with Systematic, Practical, or Pastoral Theology, or the Evidences and Study of the Bible, or Christian Missions, or Church History, or Kindred Subjects."

It is further provided that the College Committee, in conjunction with the Trustees, shall once in two years, or oftener (should exceptional circumstances render it desirable) " appoint and engage a Lecturer, who shall ordinarily be a member of the Baptist denomination, but who may occasionally be a member of any other body of Evangelical Christians, to deliver a course of not more than eight Lectures, on some subject of the nature herein before mentioned."

In accordance with these provisions, the Rev. Dr. Angus delivered, at Regent's Park College, in the year 1896, a Course of Six Lectures on *Regeneration*, afterwards published.

The sixth course, delivered in the year 1908, is contained in the present volume.

The sentences above marked as quotations are from the Deed of Trust, executed March, 1896.

CONTENTS.

	PAGE
LECTURE I.—THE RATE OF PROGRESS IN NEW TESTAMENT RESEARCH	1
LECTURE II.—THE VERDICT OF SUCCEEDING DAYS ON ANCIENT CONFLICTS	36
LECTURE III.—SOME SPECULATIONS OF TEXTUAL CRITICISM JUSTIFIED	79
LECTURE IV.—THE ROMANCE OF THE VERSIONS	111
LECTURE V.—SIDE-LIGHTS ON THE AUTHORSHIP OF THE EPISTLE TO THE HEBREWS	148
LECTURE VI.—FURTHER REFLECTIONS ON THE ART OF CONJECTURAL EMENDATION	177
LECTURE VII.—SIDE-LIGHTS FROM THE NEW TESTAMENT ON THE RELATION OF CHRISTIANITY TO THE GREEK WORLD	212

SIDE-LIGHTS ON NEW TESTAMENT RESEARCH.

LECTURE I.

THE RATE OF PROGRESS IN NEW TESTAMENT RESEARCH.

THE criticism of the New Testament is, in our day, one of the progressive sciences. It has history and it has outlook. In its history there are eras from which we reckon, in its prospect there are expectations which are of the colour of jocund day, in spite of the mist upon the mountain tops. Its record involves epoch-making discoveries which revolutionize the text, epoch-making minds which interpret the materials both new and old. "This was a great discovery," and "this was a great man," we say, in all the retrospect of genuine scientific life, and for optimism?[1] Why, there are nearly two hundred alternative readings to Matthew alone, at the foot of the pages of Westcott and Hort's New Testament after a criticism that was certainly drastic, and almost as self-confident as Bentley's. "Scarce two hundred that can deserve the least consideration!" Bentley's language reminds me of an experience of my own some thirty years ago. One of the fellows of my college came into my room one day and found me poring over the various readings in Tischendorf's New Testament. He asked me why I was wasting my time upon that: the question, said he, was settled thirty years before. The speaker was in the year of grace 2 B. H. (i.e. two years before Hort), and he assumed that the problem of the New Testament text had been settled in the year 32 B.H. If I had believed his warning, many

---

[1] Equally optimist was his reply to Collins in the famous *Remarks upon a Late Discourse of Freethinking*, "not frightened therefore with the present 30,000, I for my part, and (as I believe) many others would not lament, if out of the old manuscripts yet untouched 1,000 more were faithfully collected; some of which without question would render the text more beautiful, just and exact; though of no consequence to the main of religion, nay perhaps wholly synonymous in the view of common readers, and quite insensible in any modern version."

The Rate of Progress. 5

things would not have happened: for example, I should not be lecturing here to-day on the rate of progress in New Testament Research. But if we must not say that the text of the New Testament is settled, what are we to say of its unsettlement? Is it true that it doesn't matter; or is the unsettlement of the text like the tremors in the seismic instruments of some volcanic observatory which tell us that Vesuvius is alive and that we are going to hear from him presently?

Dr. Hort, to whom I have referred as one of the calendar men of the science, is almost as much of an optimist as Bentley, only his optimism takes a different form. He occasionally despairs of the text and suggests emendations outside the manuscript evidence; but he is quite confident that the text has never undergone heretical manipulations and that no doctrines of Christianity are affected by the investigations of the textual critic. To make sure that I do not misrepresent him I will transcribe some of his actual words:[1] " It will not be out of place to add here a distinct expression of our belief that even among the numerous unquestionably spurious readings of the New Testament there are no signs

[1] *Introduction* pp. 282—285.

of deliberate falsification for dogmatic purposes." "Accusations of wilful tampering with the text are accordingly not unfrequent in Christian antiquity; but with a single exception, wherever they can be verified they prove to be groundless, being in fact hasty and unjust inferences from mere diversities of inherited text." The one exception which Dr. Hort allows to his rule is that of the text of Marcion, who mutilated the Gospel of Luke in the interests of his own theological system. And Dr. Hort concludes with two optimistic statements: first, that "the books of the New Testament as preserved in extant documents assuredly speak to us in every important respect in language identical with that in which they spoke to those for whom they were originally written"; second, that "it would be an illusion to anticipate important changes of text from any acquisition of new evidence." A good deal has happened since those sentences were written, and much water has flowed even under the theological bridges where the currents are usually abnormally slow. It will be sufficient to say that the assumptions of textual certainty and almost final textual accuracy have not been verified, and that there is much new evidence constantly coming to light, some of which does matter not a little. Perhaps Dr. Hort's misstatement under this head is due to an error, with which he and Dr. Westcott started on their work—that the evidence was all collected and that they had only to avail themselves of the labours of their predecessors. So far, then, we find premature optimism to prevail with regard to the outcome of New Testament criticism, and premature optimism is not one of the marks of progress.

The fact is that in spite of all the work done by great and good men upon the subject, New Testament Criticism has not yet found its Newton.

That does not mean that we are not making progress, real and substantial progress. There was progress before Newton, progress after him, progress especially in him; there is progress between one Newton and the next. It is almost necessary to remind ourselves of this, because there was, and still is, especially in Cambridge circles, something like a belief that the laws of intellectual progress were suspended by Providence at the time of Dr. Hort's death, and many absurd things have been said about the finality of his analysis of the grouping of the New Testament MSS., which that acute and modest scholar would have been the first to repudiate.

Now, in order to find out what has been done in this branch of science, let us look back a little; and I suggest that a good date to look back to will be the year of grace 1881. In this year there occurred three events that were, for Englishmen at all events, of prime importance in the history of New Testament criticism: the first was the publication of the Revised Version of the New Testament;[1] the second the almost coincident[2] publication of the Greek Text of Drs. Westcott and Hort, followed by Dr. Hort's *Introduction* to the same:[3] the third was the series of articles against both the Revision and the Text contributed by Dr. Burgon to the pages of the Quarterly Review. To these three great events I add one microscopic detail from my own experience. The year 1881 is the date of

---

[1] i.e. on May 17, 1881.   [2] i.e. on May 10, 1881.

[3] Professor Sanday (*Cont. Rev.* Dec. 1881) says that the publication of the Greek Text five days before the Revised Version was an undesigned coincidence: "There seems to have been no deliberate plan in such coincidence as there was." I do not find this very convincing.

my own personal estrangement from mathematics, and conversion to criticism! The date explains my presence here to-day.

Now it is not my intention to discuss the rival merits of the Authorised and Revised Versions. The influence of the new version has been chiefly felt amongst the race of Bibliolaters, whom it has converted from Monolatry to Dilatry, from the cult of the A. V. to that of alternative A. V. and R.V., with a lesser subordinate divinity known as R.V. mg. The two versions have become a pair of heavenly twins to whom appeal is made alternately, much as the Romans used to swear *Mecastor* and *Edepol*. The instinctive desire of Protestant Christians for authoritative judgments from the book has expressed itself in the language of dilemma. I am not prepared to say that the desire is altogether wrong. It can be upheld on spiritual grounds. If we had nothing to discuss except a new translation of the sacred text, it would probably be sufficient to say that the Revised Version of the N.T. is a very bad translation and pass on. It is almost inconceivable to me that it can ever be accepted by the English-speaking people, whose language it so ruthlessly perverts. Dr. Burgon was surely right when he denounced it as follows:

"How it happened that, with so many splendid scholars sitting round their table, they (the Revisers) should have produced a Translation which, for the most part, reads like a first-rate school-boy's crib—tasteless, unlovely, harsh, unidiomatic; servile without being really faithful—pedantic without being really learned—an unreadable Translation, in short; the result of a vast amount of labour indeed, but of wondrous little skill—how all this has come about it were utterly useless at this time of day to enquire."

And I do not think that the attempts which are from time to time made to rehabilitate the Revised Version in public estimation will have any success (if indeed rehabilitation can be predicated where a position was never really occupied). The defenders of the Revised Version of the N.T. will disappear with the Revisers themselves and with those that are attached to them by what the Romans call *pietas*.[1] Dr. Weymouth's *New Testament in Modern Speech* will, perhaps, live longer. Why then do I refer to

[1] I have been struck by the way in which in certain circles the very infelicities of the Revised Version have

the Revised Version as an epoch-making event? The reason consists, not in the translation, but in the text which underlay it. Now, for the first time, the whole world of English-speaking Christians[2] was face to face with the reality and extent of the variations in the text of the New Testament. Up to the year 1881, few were aware that there were any important changes to be faced; only those who were close students,

---

become the object of devotion. For instance, I noted recently that a scholar of such excellent taste and judgment as Professor Burkitt quotes the Gospel in the form "If thy hand make thee to stumble." I also remember once taking the late Dr. Schaff ("der unermüdliche Schaff" of the Germans) to call on Dr. Westcott with a view to the removal of certain barbarisms from the Version upon which they had been engaged together; and when Dr. Westcott asked sharply for instances of the suggested improvement and reference was made to 2 Peter i. 5 ("Supply in your faith virtue, etc."), Dr. Westcott angrily replied (and it was the only occasion on which I ever saw him riding the wild horse, anger), that he would sooner cut off his right hand than alter that translation. A strange fascination for a rendering in Baboo-English of what Dr. E. A. Abbott, I believe, once called Baboo-Greek.

[2] This is what differentiates the situation from that created by the publication of Mill's New Testament, and by Dr. Bentley's proposals for the purifying of the Greek Text. They raised a very respectable storm, but it was in an academic teapot.

or who read independent translations like Dr. Davidson's translation of the text of Tischendorf, knew that the Greek text had passed into the furnace of criticism, and that it would not come out exactly the same as it went in.[1] But now on the margin of almost every page there appeared warning notes about what was to be read in "certain ancient MSS.," or in "some ancient authorities"; and the uncertainty produced by these references was accentuated by a suspicion that it was only the want of a two-thirds vote which kept such marginal matters

---

[1] Many of the rank and file read the translation of the Codex Sinaiticus which appeared as the thousandth volume of the Tauchnitz Library: the ministers, at least the more thoughtful ones of my acquaintance, read Davidson's translation of the eighth edition of Tischendorf. This last has a long introductory preface, marked by extraordinary inaccuracies uttered with great air of knowledge. I remember Ezra Abbot of Harvard (the most accurate scholar I think I have ever known), pointing out to me some of Davidson's blunders. Amongst other things he tilts at Alford's Greek Text because is was, by confession, a diplomatic text. Davidson did not know that "diploma" was another name for a manuscript, and that Alford's text professed to be based upon the manuscripts themselves. But the fact is, as Burgon loved to insinuate, very few of the Revisers even, who set themselves to re-construct the New Testament Text, had ever handled or collated a codex for themselves.

The Rate of Progress. 13

out of the text itself.[1] And whatever suspicions were aroused were confirmed by the controversy which arose and the battle royal which prevailed over the merits of the Revision generally. Injudicious Revisers began to tell the secrets of their prison-house, and in a very little while the Christian Church was taking sides for or against this or that rendering. Emerson described the spiritual temper of his time as "a whole generation of gentlemen and ladies out in search of a religion;" and so here a whole generation of Christian people were out in search of a correct theory of the text of the New Testament. And when we reflect how difficult it is to get any but experts to take an interest in matters which everyone ought to know something about, I think that, if the Revisers did nothing more than to force the attention of Christian people to the origins of the Christian documents, they accomplished a great result, and so produced an epoch-making work—though not in the way that they intended. The chief value of the Revision therefore consists in the Greek text which underlies it. This is, to

---

[1] A vote of one-third of the revisers present in favour of a reading of the Authorised Version was sufficient to secure it from disturbance.

a very large extent, the revised text of Westcott and Hort, copies of which were confidentially placed, in advance of publication, in the hands of all the revisers, and the merits of which could be defended and explained by the presence of the skilled editors themselves who had produced it. Thus when the Revised New Testament appeared, every Christian reader had to face such questions as to what was the real ending of Mark's Gospel, and whether Jesus really prayed for His enemies upon the Cross.

So much, in passing, with regard to the Revised Version. Our next business is with the text of Westcott and Hort and with the criticisms which it provoked from Dr. Burgon. Now apart from the merits of the two sides in this great controversy it is matter of satisfaction that the publication and discussion of the Westcott and Hort text demonstrated that English Scholarship was to the front in the matter of textual criticism. For a time it seemed as if Germany had ceased to take an interest in the subject. Her Biblical students had moved into other fields. Tischendorf had left no successor in his native country and he had never lived to write the Prolegomena which were to justify the text of his eighth edition. No such work as Hort's *Introduction* had ever appeared in Germany, nor was there anyone in Germany who was able to bring a knowledge of Patristic quotations to bear upon the criticism of the text in the way that Burgon did, on almost every page of his Quarterly Review articles. For once, English scholars were leading the world; and when they fought, the rest of the world looked on and did not venture to intervene, so as to draw off attention from the main combatants. It need hardly be said that this state of things could not last. The Germans are not long outside the knowledge of any great question, and their apparent isolation was but temporary. They are now amongst the keenest of textual critics, and under the leadership of Professor Nestle, Professor Gregory, and Professor von Soden are rapidly restoring the balance of power. Here is a significant bit of evidence given me by one of my German friends. A few years since one of the most famous German Universities possessed a copy of Scrivener's edition of the Cambridge manuscript, known as the Codex Bezae, which was unused and, I believe, uncut. To-day it is out of its covers from constant reference and handling. That will serve for a parable of how the tide of textual criticism is coming in again in Germany, and I think we may say that it has not altogether ebbed in England. So, if national pride be ever lawful, here is a field in which it may be indulged. Only there is a caution to be expressed with regard to our temporary primacy in this field. We did not deserve any such pre-eminence, in view of the fact that our great Universities had practically limited research in this subject to those who are not members of the Established Church by closing professorships to those who are not members of that Church. *A nation which elects to live on half its brains has no right to expect to rule the world.* And until learning is de-clericalised we cannot expect to reach or to retain the highest standards. It is surprising that no English Government sees this; or perhaps we ought to say it is surprising that the English people do not see it. We may hope that our great Universities, as is said of Wisdom generally, will be justified of their children: but they do harm, by their narrowness, to the subjects that they profess to teach.

The Revised Version appeared on May 17th, 1881, and within the space of a few days was

The Rate of Progress. 17

followed by the Greek Text of Westcott and Hort. In the month of August appears the famous *Introduction* of Dr. Hort: and in the Quarterly Review for October the first of the articles by Dr. Burgon, afterwards incorporated in the volume entitled *The Revision Revised*. Dr. Burgon tells us in the published volume that he had been working on the first of his articles all through the long summer days of 1881, and that when the October number of the Quarterly Review appeared he knew that the new Greek Text (and therefore the new English Version) had "received its death-blow. It might for a few years drag out a maimed existence; eagerly defended by some—timidly pleaded for by others. But such efforts could be of no avail. Its days were already numbered, . . ." These words were written two years after the first appearance of the Revised Version; they certainly are not destitute of self-confidence. They announce that two big birds had been killed, I will not say with one stone, but with one mitrailleuse. So it becomes proper to ask whether Burgon had really done these two things, destroyed the Greek Text of the later critics, and the English Revision which was built to a large extent, upon it. With regard to the English Revision, I should, as intimated above, make a fairly complete surrender—not on account of its underlying Greek Text so much as on account of its infelicitous renderings of any text at all. I think, too, that it should be conceded that Burgon was right in saying that none of those who had attempted to reply to him had answered his arguments. A glance over the pamphlets which were produced on the other side will show what I mean. Canon Farrar attacked Burgon in the Contemporary Review,[1] and assured him that "The Quarterly Reviewer can be refuted as fully as he desires as soon as any scholar has the leisure to answer him." That means that Farrar had tried to answer him and found the matter outside either his time or his capacity. He was no match for Burgon in

---

[1] March, 1882. Farrar was astonishingly feeble, and often very loose in his statements. How does it look in the light of to-day to pen a sentence like this: "Not only has our general knowledge of the Greek language become far more accurate than it was at any previous period, but the specialities of the Hellenistic dialect have been thoroughly mastered by the labours of many successive grammarians and lexicographers." What would Deissmann, Moulton and the papyrologists say to this?

The Rate of Progress. 19

Textual Criticism or in vituperation. Burgon calls the article a "Vulgar effusion," says that his "remarks are hysterical," assures him that "The Quarterly Reviewer can afford to wait—if the Revisers can; but they are reminded that it was no answer to one who has demolished their Master's 'Theory,' for the pupils to keep on reproducing fragments of it; and by their mistakes and exaggerations, to make both themselves and him ridiculous." You will notice the singular "him" in that last sentence, and the reference to the "Master;" Burgon knew well enough that it was Hort with whom he had to contend, not even Westcott and Hort. He treated the rest of them as so many buzzing flies, and went on rattling his challenge on the shield of Achilles, Achilles meanwhile keeping in his tent. It was the same with nearly all the other antagonists. They cut a sorry figure, because of their want of acquaintance with the subject; even Dr. Kennedy said nothing that had any bearing on the debate,[1] and Dr. Sanday barely

---

[1] Dr. Kennedy's knowledge of the problem as compared with Burgon's may be seen from the following estimate of the materials for the determination of the text. *Ely Lectures on the Revised Version*, p. xliv. "We find also

touched the edge of the controversy.[2] An exception, however, arose when Dr. Ellicott, the Chairman of the Revision, volunteered to defend with another of the Revisers, a selected position, viz: the change of the reading in I Tim. iii. 16 ("God was manifest in the flesh"), as well as to vindicate generally the textual theory of Dr. Hort, and the consequent primacy of the Vatican Codex over all other MSS. of the N.T. On looking over this controversy again (and I was interested in it at the time, because I ventured to offer Dr.

---

some assistance in the passages of Scripture cited by Christian writers of the earliest ages especially by those who are usually called Fathers of the Church." "Some assistance"!

[2] His acquaintance with the subject at that time was not what it is to-day. Like the rest of us, I suspect, he was learning of Westcott and Hort and learning fast. He admits as much at the close of his article in the Contemporary Review. "As I have come forward in defence of their principles it is perhaps right that I should explain the degree of my own indebtedness to them. . . . I am not prepared to claim (for myself at least) more than certain rough results, which a deeper knowledge may perhaps somewhat modify." A sentence marked by Sandayan indecision—and modesty. Where Sanday was decided, he was almost certainly wrong, as in the statement that we were all agreed as to the worthlessness of the Western readings.

Ellicott some MS. confirmations, from my own collations, of certain of his references), it is impossible to resist the conclusion that Dr. Ellicott was wholly outclassed. Burgon knew it, and told him so plainly with savage candour, and his usual skill in vituperation. How will this do for candour? " Forgive my plainness, but really you are so conspicuously unfair—and at the same time so manifestly unacquainted (except at second-hand and only in an elementary way) with the points actually under discussion—that, were it not for the adventitious importance attaching to any utterance of yours, deliberately put forth at this time as Chairman of the New Testament body of Revisers, I should have taken no notice of your pamphlet." To which piece of candid criticism may be added the following insinuations of want of competence in matters that belong to the expert. " Did you ever take the trouble to collate a Sacred Manuscript? If you ever did, pray with what did you make your collation?" " From the confident style in which you deliver yourself upon such matters, and especially from your having undertaken to preside over a Revision of the Sacred Text, one would suppose that at some period of your life you must have given the subject a considerable amount of time and attention." And when Burgon had finished his bout with the Bishop, it must be admitted that he had vastly strengthened the case for the received text in I Tim. iii. 16, for which he gathered up no less than 300 MSS. witnesses, and any amount of Patristic testimony, some carried over bodily from his opponents. It is time for me to state that I believe he was entirely wrong in his conclusions, but it is impossible to ignore the vigour of his onslaught or the range of his artillery. He had spent five and a half years collating the five great ancient MSS. throughout the Gospels,[1] and a man who had done that had a right to speak with conviction, even if he were not altogether right. Moreover he had accomplished the gigantic task of searching the Fathers for all the passages which they quote from the New Testament and the results of this labour are preserved in a long series of index volumes now in the British Museum. It is possible to object to many of his references and to find fault with some of the texts which he used, but I

[1] I happen to possess his copy of the Roman Edition of the Vatican Codex.

The Rate of Progress. 23

only wish that I possessed a transcript of those precious volumes. They were the magazine from which he drew his thunders in the Quarterly Review, to the amazement alike of his friends and enemies.

How was it then that no one answered Burgon? Well there were not more than two or three who could have done it. A person who wanted to floor Burgon would have done well to begin with his earlier book in defence of the last twelve verses of Mark. Here is a case in which Burgon was undoubtedly wrong, but his defence of the conventional text was so vigorous and so adroit, that he held the position for a quarter of a century after he ought to have abandoned it. Not a few critics, such as Samuel Davidson and the like, tried to dislodge him, but theirs was mere pea-shooting. And as far as English scholarship goes, nothing really vital was said until Hort wrote the long note at the end of his Introduction,[1] which people at once recognised to be the counterplea to Burgon. And that note was so closely abbreviated and so inaccessible to the ordinary reader that I

[1] He had already come forward on the question in an article in the *Academy*.

doubt if it made many converts. Some one should certainly have written a volume directly, as a reply to Burgon's arguments; the subject demanded and deserved a separate treatment, and it would have been a splendid training ground for one of the younger scholars of the day. Why did they not do it? Why did we not do it ourselves? Our lot might have been worse!

But as regards the Quarterly Review articles, there were not many, as I have said, who could have ventured into the arena. Dr. Westcott made an attempt to galvanize the corpse of the Revised Version into fresh life, by writing a little book on its merits, which could hardly prove a reply to those who were occupied with its defects. And when he came in 1896 to re-issue the *Introduction*, after Dr. Hort's death, he made the following statement with regard to the controversies which had prevailed. " No arguments have been advanced against the general principles maintained in the Introduction and illustrated in the Notes, since the publication of the first edition, which were not fully considered by Dr. Hort and myself in the long course of our work and in our judgment dealt with

The Rate of Progress. 25

adequately." One can scarcely call that a reply. It is only an "Ipse dixi" in the dual.[1]

There was one man, who could have held and handled Burgon, had already done it on a minor point; I mean Dr. Ezra Abbot, of Harvard. I remember writing to him on the subject, and asking him whether a reply was not demanded by these articles in the Quarterly, and I find amongst my letters his reply to my hint dated October 22, 1883: "I agree that Burgon has not been thoroughly answered; but I have no space or time now to give my view of the matter. His book entitled the 'Revision Revised,' a reprint with some modifications of the three articles in the Quarterly, enlarged, with the addition of a reply to the two Revisers, was announced as on the eve of publication a month or six weeks ago, and even the number of pages in the book was given in the advertise-

---

[1] There is a precisely similar evasion of criticism on the part of Westcott in his *Lessons of the Revised Version*, pp. 2, 3. "They [the Revisers] heard in the Jerusalem Chamber all the arguments against their conclusions which they have heard since; and I may say for myself, that no amount of restatement of old arguments has in the least degree shaken my confidence in the general results that were obtained."

ment; but I do not know that it has yet been issued." From which it appears that Ezra Abbot was too busy to take the matter up. But what, you will ask, of Achilles himself? Why did not Hort come out into the open field and settle the questions at issue, much in the same way as Bentley settled Boyle over the letters of Phalaris? I remember asking him once a question on this point; but, if I remember rightly the reasons that he gave for his silence they resolved themselves into questions of etiquette. First of all, Dr. Burgon had never sent him a copy of his articles; and second, if I understood his allusion rightly, he suspected that someone had divulged to Burgon the Greek text of the N.T. which had been submitted to him in confidence as a Reviser—a proceeding which would naturally have provoked resentment, although it is difficult to see how a secret of such magnitude could have been kept for so long by so many people. As far as my memory goes that is all the explanation which Dr. Hort could or would give me. One is not bound, I suppose, to reply to every attack made upon himself or his positions; otherwise some of us would have a sorry life. One may elect to await the verdict of time, and let one's adversary

The Rate of Progress. 27

crow in triumph over one's apparent acquiescence. Burgon, himself, quick as he was to snatch at the laurels of apparent victory, had a word from the inward monitor on the other side. In his reply to Ellicott he quotes a famous maxim from Pindar:

'Ἀμέραι δ' ἐπίλοιποι μάρτυρες σοφώτατοι.

"That their views (i.e. those of Westcott and Hort) have been received with expressions of the greatest disapprobation, no one will deny. Indispensable to their contention is the grossly improbable hypothesis that the Peschito is to be regarded as the 'Vulgate' (i.e. the *Revised*) Syriac: Cureton's, as the 'Vetus' or original Syriac version. And yet, while I write, the Abbé Martin at Paris is giving it as the result of his labours on this subject, that Cureton's version cannot be anything of the sort. Whether Westcott and Hort's theory of a '*Syrian*' text has not received an effectual quietus, let posterity decide."

Then follows the quotation from Pindar. And what has posterity decided? The "grossly improbable hypothesis" has been confirmed in the strongest manner, by the discovery of a further old Syriac MS., and a mass of accessory evidence; the Abbé Martin's pamphlet was written when he was under intellectual aberration, and the less said about it the better; and the argument of Westcott and Hort can hardly be said to have received a quietus at all. So, as Abbot refused to reply to Burgon, and Achilles did not come out of his tent, let us keep our eyes fixed upon the remnant of the days and watch what further light is going to break on the interesting field of controversy. If you like, let us say that neither party took the laurel of victory, though one vociferously claimed it: we will leave them encamped upon the field, and see in what directions reinforcements are coming up for the conclusion of the conflict.[1]

---

[1] On looking over some old letters belonging to the eighties, I find a sheaf from Dr. Burgon showing the greatest interest in the work which I was doing, and giving me some of the wisest counsels as to how to concentrate my power of study and what to concentrate upon. I believe that we remained good friends to the last, and I am sure that I learned much by the direct intercourse which I had with him. It is very pleasant to remember this in the case of those whom we have sometimes remorselessly criticised.

APPENDIX TO LECTURE I.

In the foregoing lecture I have alluded to the astonishingly optimistic statements which Dr. Hort made with regard to the preservation of the New Testament from hostile and heretical influences. The only exception which he allowed was that of Marcion's readings, which consisted mainly in excisions from the text of Luke, made with a view to the removal of everything which would involve the New Testament Christian in the belief in the God of the Old Testament. Now even when Dr. Hort makes the admission that Marcion mutilated the N. T. with a heretical intention, he does not seem to think that this made any difference to the evangelical tradition, but I should say that even in the matter of Marcionism Hort was too optimistic.

We know that Marcion had no Infancy Sections in his Gospel. Perhaps he had removed them because he did not wish to recognise a fulfilment of prophecy. He had no Infancy Sections because from his point of view, there was no Infancy. Christ had descended suddenly into the synagogue (everything was sudden with Marcion, says Tertullian) and began His work at once. Now it stands to reason that no such opinion could be held if the Gospel of Luke, as we know it, had been held at the same time. I am not speaking of the chapters describing the Infancy, but of the passage which tells that our Lord came to Nazareth *where He had been brought up*, and went into the synagogue *according to His custom*. Naturally Tertullian could at once retort upon his Marcionite antagonist and question as to how the custom arose for a person who had only just arrived. And it could only be answered by the Marcionite method of excision. Either the word *His* must be erased before custom, or the whole clause must go. If, therefore, we find the compromising words absent in a MS. it raises the suspicion of Marcionite corruption. What do we actually find? One of the most famous old Latin MS. (the Palatine Codex) has lost the clause about " His custom " altogether. The Codex Bezae omits the word " His," and is followed by two other Latin MSS.

of the first rank. Further the Codex Bezae omits the clause as to our Lord's having been brought up in Nazareth, and simply says that He came into the synagogue. Is not that sufficient to suggest Marcionism in the current texts of Luke, and ought we not to recognise it, both in Luke iv. 16 and elsewhere. And will it be sufficient, on the other hand, to re-assure people and say that no harm has been done and that no one ever had a vicious intention in transcription or preparation of texts? For it will not be possible to refer all changes of this kind to Marcion himself. They are due to a school as well as to a master. And if one school can alter the text, why not another? What is true of the influence of the Marcionite movement upon the text is also true of the contemporary heresy of Encratism. If Marcion affected the text, are we entitled to say that Tatian never affected it? We know now that his compound Gospel, the Diatessaron, became for a time the standard Gospel in the Syrian Church, and that it profoundly influenced the text of the separate Gospels. Is it to be assumed that on questions like the eating of animal food, the drinking of wine, the virtue of celibacy, and the like, we are to believe that no Encratisms appear in the text? A little enquiry will soon enlighten us. We know now that Tatian along with many early believers was sorely puzzled by the presence of the locusts in the diet of that very holy man, John the Baptist. One school, probably those who pass under the name of Nazarenes or Ebionites, changed the Greek name of locusts ἀκρίδες into the similarly sounding word ἐγκρίδες, "pancakes" for "locusts." But Tatian was bolder than this, he removed the locusts, and gave St. John a diet of "milk and honey" in place of the conventional *menu*. This meant Encratism in the text. And there must have been much more of it, for we find traces of similar corrections in the oldest Syriac MSS. that are known to us. In the Lewis MS., for example, we find the "oxen and fatlings" removed from the supper of the King in Matt. xx. 4: and we find the period of married life of that holy woman, the prophetess Anna (Luke ii. 36), reduced from seven years' felicity to a bare seven days. These instances may suffice to show how the religious movements of any time or country affect the text of that time or country. Nor can such changes be considered as unimportant or insignificant. We find the question of the re-action of Ebionite or Adoptionist views raised (or of Anti-Ebionite or Anti-Adoptionist corrections) as soon as we study the second-century textual variations in the light of the history of doctrine in the second century. Suppose, for example, we were studying Justin Martyr's *Dialogue with Trypho the Jew*, we should find Trypho expostulating with Justin over the titles that he gives to Jesus Christ. Trypho is ready, or almost ready, for the expression of some faith in Christ, but he enters a protest against Justin's way of putting it. He objects to the Virgin Birth as being comparable to the Greek legend of Perseus: Justin ought to be ashamed to say such things, and it would be much better to regard Christ as a man sprung from human origin, who on account of His law-abiding and perfect life was elected to be the Messiah: (κατηξιῶσθαι ἐκλεγῆναι εἰς Χριστόν.)[1] A little later Justin returned to the point, and asked Trypho with regard to his admission that, on account of his life in accordance with the law of Moses, Jesus had been *elected* to be the Messiah. You can see an Ebionite watchword protruding through the dialogue, and this means

[1] Justin, *Dial.* 67.

that in the second century there was a Judaeo-Christian party which called Christ, not the Son of God, but the Elect of God. Is that reflected on the text of the New Testament? An examination of the oldest witnesses will show abundantly that there has been either

(a) An unlawful insertion of the title ἐκλεκτός or ἐκλελεγμένος into the text of a number of passages; or else

(b) There has been an unlawful erasure of the same term (which is one of the pre-Christian names for the Messiah), in the interests of a progressive Christology.

This is not the place to discuss the point at length, but it may suffice to show that Dr. Hort cannot be right in divesting the various readings of New Testament MSS. of dogmatic significance, or in assuring us of the universal *bona fides* of the transcribers. His statement on these points must remain an astonishment to us, but perhaps enough has been said to show why we were not able to agree with his optimistic views of the textual history.

For a more balanced judgment we may compare what my friend, the late Professor Berger, wrote in regard to the text of the

Latin Vulgate (*Hist. de la Vulgate*, p. viii.):

"La dogmatique elle-même a sans doute une grand part de responsabilité dans la corruption du texte de la Bible Latine. . . . Les alterations dogmatiques, en effet, ne sont pas rares dans le texte de la Vulgate. . . . Les doctrines les plus chères aux théologiens du moyen âge exercent toutes leur influence sur le texte de la Bible. Ici c'est le dogme de la Trinité, que l'on veut trouver formulé en toutes lettres dans la Bible et que l'on affirme par la fameuse interpolation du passage des trois temoins! C'est la foi en la divinité de Jésus-Christ qui s'exprime en un grand nombre de falsifications de détail, toujours au détriment de son humanité."

What is true of the Vulgate is true of the Greek texts which preceded it. But to Dr. Hort the scribes were all angels, as far as theology was concerned.

LECTURE II.

The Verdict of Succeeding Days on Ancient Conflicts.

IN our previous lecture we were discussing the situation which was created in the year 1881 by the issue of the Revised Version, and the publication of the New Greek Text of Westcott and Hort. We saw how hotly both the translation and the underlying text were assailed by Dr. Burgon, and how he held his ground against all comers, and serenely awaited the judgment of the " remnant of the days " ('Αμέραι ἐπίλοιποι). As it is nearly thirty years since that great battle was first joined, and we may, therefore, ourselves be fairly regarded as chronologically identified with the Court of Appeal, it will be interesting to examine what we think of the issue now. Suppose that those Quarterly Review articles had just appeared in October, 1908, instead of in October, 1881, could they present the same confident demeanour as on their actual appearance? We will make an experiment and see what will happen. The first case that Dr. Burgon brings forward will be found on p. 5 of his *Revision Revised* and runs as follows:

"Undeniable at all events it is, that the effect which these ever-recurring announcements [of the existence of various readings] produce on the devout reader of Scripture, is the reverse of edifying; is never helpful; is always bewildering. A man of ordinary acuteness can but exclaim—'Yes, very likely. But *what of it*?' My eye happens to alight on 'Bethesda' (in St. John v. 2): against which I find in the margin, 'Some ancient authorities read *Bethsaida*, others *Bethzatha*.' Am I then to understand that in the judgment of the Revisionists it is uncertain which of those three names is right? . . . Not so the expert, who is overheard to moralize concerning the phenomena of the case after a less ceremonious fashion. '"*Bethsaida!*" yes the Old Latin[1] and the Vulgate,[2] countenanced by *one* manuscript of bad character, so reads.

[1] Tertullian *bis*.
[2] Hieron Opp. ii. 177 c. (see the note).

"*Bethzatha*!" yes, the blunder is found in *two* manuscripts, both of bad character. Why do you not go on to tell us that *another* manuscript exhibits "*Belzetha*"? Another (supported by Eusebius[1] and [in one place] by Cyril,[2] "*Bezatha*"? Nay, why not say plainly that there are found to *exist upwards of thirty* blundering representations of this same word; but that "*Bethesda*"—the reading of sixteen uncials and the whole body of the cursives, besides the Peschito and Cureton's Syriac, the Armenian, Georgian and Slavonic versions—Didymus,[3] Chrysostom,[4] and Cyril[5])—is the only reasonable way of exhibiting it; to speak plainly, *why encumber your margin with such a note at all?*' . . But we are moving forward too fast."

From the foregoing statement you will see that the judgment of the Revisers was divided between the three readings *Bethesda*, *Bethsaida* and *Bethzatha*. Of these, they kept *Bethesda* in the text and referred to *Bethsaida* and *Bethzatha* on the margin. The rest of the possible readings they neglected: there is no need for

[1] Hieron iii. 121.
[2] iv. 617 c. ed Pusey.
[3] p. 272.
[4] i. 548 c; viii. 207 a.
[5] iv. 205.

The Verdict of Succeeding Days. 39

us to go into the jungle after them at present. It is sufficient to remember that for our purposes in the first instance we have to keep before our minds the three forms, Bethesda, Bethsaida and Bethzatha. The first is the reading of the Received Text, the second is the reading of the Vatican Codex (Cod. B),[1] the third is the reading of the Sinai Codex (known as cod. ℵ). The last two MSS. are said to be MSS. of bad character, and as these two manuscripts are those which are commonly followed, the one by Dr. Hort, the other by Dr. Tischendorf, we may say, if we like, that it is a choice between three editors, Burgon, Hort and Tischendorf, of whom the two last are men of bad character, because they persist in following MSS. of bad character.[2] As I say, we do not need to go into the jungle for more readings at present, but if we did, Dr. Burgon

---

[1] It will be confirmed presently from one of the Egyptian MSS. recently acquired by Mr. Freer of Detroit.

[2] How decided were Burgon's views with regard to the great Uncials may be illustrated from a marginal note in his copy of the edition of the Codex Zacynthius, now in my possession: Tregelles had pointed out (p. iii.) the kind of text presented by the Codex, and its affinity with the very best codices. Upon this Burgon writes "I should have said the very worst!"

would cut our way out on the line that may be described as the Consentient Testimony of Catholic Antiquity.

When we turn to Dr. Hort's text, we find that he does not actually put the reading of the Vatican MS. into the text; he puts the Sinai reading in the text and the other in the foot-note or margin, but it is quite clear that he really wants to put the B-reading into the text if it can be done. For if you look at his note on the subject (*Notes on Select Readings*, p. 76) you will see that he definitely states that *Bethsaida* may be right, as it is supported by B. and a great variety of versions, and he suggests that the name means *House of Fish* and might be very appropriately given to a tank hewn in the rock. For convenience of reference I will add the whole of his note.

"John v. 2 : Βηθζαθά (Marg.) Βηθσαιδά b.c. vg. me (Βηδσ. cod. opt.) the (Βηδσ). Syr. hl. txt. mg. gr. actl. (Βηθασα.) Tert. Βηθεσδά. Syrian (Gr. Lat. [it] Syr. Arm. incl. Did. Text ℵ 33 (*rhe*) also Βηζαθά Le. Eus. *Onom.*; also Βελζεθά D (a), *Betzatha* (*ata,— eta*) b. f. vg. Codd: hence—ζ—θα, ℵ L. D. 33 lat. vt. Eus.

Text and margin are but slight modifications of the same name; and perhaps its purest form would be Βηθζαιθά, *The House of the Olive.* Βηθσαιδά may however be right, as it is supported by B. and a great variety of vv:[1] a tank hewn in the rock might naturally bear the name *House of Fish.*"

Here we have a pretty bit of jungle, of the kind which commonly occurs in Textual Criticism: the sum total of it is that Dr. Hort unceremoniously rejects the verdict of Catholic Antiquity; would like to follow the Vatican MS., actually follows the Sinaitic MS. with Tischendorf, and explains the two names which he prefers on their Hebrew etymologies. There then you have the two opposing critics locked horn in horn in fight, and the question is what do the succeeding days say about the probable issue of the combat between these two strong bulls of Bashan?

Now suppose we leave the textual theorists on one side, and begin investigating the question without any knowledge, in the first instance, of the special MSS. involved, only knowing that the name of the pool has come down to us in a variety of forms, and wishing to find out something about it. So we begin by asking

[1] i.e. the Egyptian and Ethiopic Versions follow Cod. B.

questions of the simplest kind that curiosity can suggest. What is this *Bethesda*, or whatever its name may be? The answer is, that it is a pool in Jerusalem. How do we know that? Because the Gospel of John opens its fifth chapter by saying that there is in Jerusalem a certain pool with an uncertain name. Is the pool yet extant? The answer is, we do not know; that is, we do not know in the year 1881. We may perhaps know in succeeding days. Is there any way of knowing? Are there any marks of identification? Yes, it is said to be near the Sheep-something: but we cannot make out whether it is Sheep-gate or Sheep-pool or Sheep-market. Do we know of any Sheep-gate in Jerusalem? Only from references in Nehemiah, which appear to place such a gate in the North Wall of the city, near the East End. Do we know of any Sheep-pool? Not the least. Have we any other identification? Yes, it is said to have five porches or arches. Is there any pool in Jerusalem that is flanked by five arches? Not that we know of in the year of grace 1881. Has any one seen this pool since the time when this event happened, or since it was recorded to have happened? Yes, it was seen amongst others by a certain pilgrim from Bordeaux in the year 333 A.D. What does he say of it? He says that "inside the city there are a pair of pools, having five arches, which pools are called Betsaida."[1] May not this have been a reckless identification on the part of a pious traveller? Reckless identification would hardly produce five arches. Then may we say the real name of the pool is Bethsaida? No, we may only say that the Bordeaux pilgrim called it so. He may have taken the name from his Gospel, and the double pool with the five arches from his observation. But in that case have we not conceded the form of the name, by a second piece of evidence coeval with the Vatican Codex, and does not this virtually settle the question? No, for Eusebius, writing about the same time, and with excellent means of knowing, calls it Bezatha. Then what are we to do to settle the question? I thought we were going to wait the wise testimony of succeeding days.

Suppose then we transfer ourselves to the city of Jerusalem in the year 1888, and examine the excavations which the Roman Catholic monks

[1] "interius vero civitati sunt piscinae gemellares, quinque porticus habentes, quae appellantur Betsaida."

are making in the neighbourhood of the Church of St. Anne in the N.E. corner of the city. They have brought to light the remains of an ancient church, and here is a stairway leading down to a crypt under the church, or perhaps it is an earlier church. On the N. wall of the crypt there are the remains of an ancient fresco, and we can clearly see the figure of an angel; the figure is crossed by wavy lines of a conventional character which represent water, and it is clear that what is commemorated is the troubling of the water by the descent of the angel into it. We ought, therefore, to be somewhere in the neighbourhood of the famous pool. But this is not all. The wall of the crypt is divided into five compartments, which imitate arches. So there can be no doubt that this is the Bethesda Church. Carry the excavation under the floor of the crypt, and a further flight of steps takes you down to the pool itself, and to five shallow porticoes on its north side, lying underneath the imitation arches of the floor above. Here, then, we have what seemed to me when I first saw it,[1] shortly after the exposure of the fresco and the discovery of the pool, the best piece of archæo-

[1] In January, 1889.

logical identification that has yet been made in Jerusalem. The site seems to have been lost under the rubbish of the N.E. quarter of the city from very early times, and has been sought by pilgrims and travellers and scholars in every conceivable corner of the city. The accuracy of the identification rests upon the five arches which flank the pool; it can hardly be maintained that these are an artificial product of a pious church-builder, who thought he had found Bethesda, for the pious builder evidently imitated what he had already found. Nor is there any suggestion on the part of the Bordeaux pilgrim that a church had been built over the pool at the time of his visit, though the arches, or at least the ruins of them, were there already.[1]

We may fairly claim, then, that the pool has been found, and in all probability the sheep-gate can be identified somewhere in the same angle

---

[1] Dr. Mommert *Der Teich Bethesda* pp. 34, argues that the Bordeaux Pilgrim did not see the five arches, but simply took them from the text: for, he says, Eusebius in his Onomasticon says that the Bethesda Pool is the probatic [i.e. sheep-] pool, formerly having five arches. And Jerome in his translation of Eusebius says that the pool had five arches formerly. But all of this is quite consistent with the theory that the ruins of the arches and their ancient foundations could be clearly made out.

of Jerusalem, as suggested by the references in Nehemiah. But what are we to call the pool? To answer this question, look at any map of the Holy City and you will find the quarter in which the pool has been located is known by the name of Bezetha. The name is so much like the forms which are given in the critical apparatus to John v. 2, that it will be worth our while to study the name that is written across the N.E. angle of the map of Jerusalem. It is curious that so few have seen the meaning of this striking coincidence of names. In the edition of the Itinerary of the Bordeaux Pilgrim published by the Palestine Pilgrims' Text Society, Sir Charles Wilson notes that the name Bezetha, by which Josephus distinguishes the hill north of the Temple, is merely a different form of Bethzatha; and that it may be suggested as possible that the pool derived its name from the hill and was known as the "Pool of Bethzatha." And in a note he argues that "as far as reasons of language go Βεζεθά, Βῆζαθά, Βηθζαθά, etc. may be different forms of the same word. Dr. Mommert suggests hesitatingly that Eusebius changed the name of the pool from Bethesda to Bezatha, in order to define the pool by the quarter of the city where it is found: but he does not follow up the clue. Eusebius had no need to make any change. The names were the same. Conder also came near the identification in Hastings' *Dictionary* where he notes: " In א and L the name is given as *Bethzatha* (comp. the name of Bezetha for the north quarter of Jerusalem); in B. it is Bethsaida." The comparison would have been better, if he had given the real reading of L., which is *Bezatha*. But evidently the point had not seriously impressed him, for he goes on to say that " a more probable site for Bethesda is the Virgin's Pool ... at the foot of the Ophel slope south-east of the Temple as proposed by Robinson," from which it appears that he did not attach serious weight when he wrote the article to the Bethesda excavations.[1] It is curious that he pays so little attention to them.

Why, then, do we call this corner of the city

---

[1] In the account of the re-discovery of the Pool given in Quarterly Statement of the Palestine Exploration Fund for 1888, Conder has a note and calls it the Mediæval Pool of Bethesda. He says that it is doubtful whether it can claim to be the real Bethesda, and talks of the Virgin's fountain. Why the Pilgrim of Bordeaux and Eusebius should be called Mediæval does not appear.

Bezetha? The answer is that we take it from Josephus, to whose pages we must now turn, in order to verify the spelling etc. We shall find then in Josephus' *Wars of the Jews*, five passages in which he describes the elevated ground on the north of the Temple and beyond the Tower of Antonia by the name in question. He tells us that it was separated from the Castle of Antonia by a deep fosse, and that the Timber Market was in the neighbourhood, and he explains to us the meaning of the name. Let us look at the MSS. of Josephus, to see whether there are any variations in the spelling, for there is a critical apparatus to Josephus, as well as to the Gospel of John. We at once discover that many of the same variations turn up which were noted by Burgon and Hort. For instance we have Betheza, Bethaza, Bezetha, Bethzetha, Bethesdan, Besdethan, Besdathan, Bethsaidam, Bezethana and Zebethana, with some even worse aberrations; i.e., we have a series which is very like what we have in John; and it seems clear that the aberrations are due to the same or similar causes, and they can be reduced to the same types as in the Gospel. Fortunately the text of Josephus is not under the care of Catholic Antiquity, in the way that Burgon supposes the N.T. to be; and we are therefore at liberty to say that no sane critic would edit the name in Josephus as *Bethesda* or as *Bethsaida*; the only alternatives being *Betheza* and *Bezetha*, or slight modifications of these. I notice that Niese, the latest editor, does not insist that the same spelling should rule throughout Josephus, but edits now *Betheza*, now *Bethezan*, now *Bezetha*, and *Bezatha*. The real spelling seems to me to be one of these forms. Now if this is what Josephus calls the quarter of the city, and the same name is given to the pool in the Codex L., the probability is that Codex L. has best preserved the original name, which is very close indeed to what Hort edited, evidently against his will. So we shall say that the name of the pool is *Betheza* or *Bezetha*.

But then there is another point of interest which comes up out of our observation of the coincident readings and variations in Josephus and in John. We know also, from Josephus, the meaning of the name. For instance he tells us in one place (B.J. ii. 530) that "Cestius burned the Bezetha or *Newtown*, and the Timber Market and then encamped over against the King's Palace," (i.e. the Antonia). In another passage (B.J. v. 151) he tells us that " in the language of the district the recently built quarter of the city was called *Bezetha* which you may translate into Greek as New Town or Kainopolis."[1] Here again we see how both Burgon and Hort are at fault: Burgon by supporting *Bethesda* which means *House of Mercy*, Hort by suggesting *House of the Olive* or *House or Place of Fish*. It must be quite clear by this time that the name Bethsaida has wandered from the real Fish-Town on the Lake of Galilee: the reading of the Vatican Codex is certainly wrong. As to the other forms, there is something to be said for Bethesda, if we abandon the meaning commonly given to it, and regard the spelling as an attempt to express more accurately what Josephus tells us is the true meaning. For it is clear that he is working on the two Hebrew words *Beth* which means " a house " and *Ḥadash* which means " new." And just as he makes *Qadesh* into the Greek *Kedasa*, so he has made *Newtown* into *Bethedesa* from which *Betheza* is a more rapid pronunciation. But it should be noticed that the *Bethesda* of the Received Text is very near, after all, to what must have been the

[1] So also in B.J. v. 246.

original Hebrew.[1] Probably then it is an editorial refinement on the part of some early reviser and a very good one. This then is what the succeeding days have to say on the subject of the name of the Pool: both the great antagonists were wrong, Hort badly wrong, and Burgon very slightly. But we have found the Pool and are very near indeed to its name. So far, so good.

But now, after we have gained a little light on an obscure problem, without, as we hope, being unduly tedious, may we leave the great warriors on one side and examine into some other questions relating to this very interesting section of John. It will be noticed that we have already done the Fourth Evangelist a very good turn; we have vindicated his geographical accuracy in a very important particular. Now let us go

---

[1] It is an interesting study to trace in the Old Testament the transliterations of the O.T. names by the various scribes and translators. For instance, in Judges vi. 25 the text of B. has Esdri (Ἐσδρεί) where the text of A. has Ἰεζρί (Yezri). Both transliterations are an attempt to render a Hebrew Zayin. So that in this literature we may equate the sd and z without difficulty. In the same way most MSS. and translators will render Ezra by Esdras, and there is no need to assume the d to be intrusive.

on and see if we can vindicate his history.[1] As you probably know, there has been great controversy over the first verse of this fifth chapter of John, and the reference in it to a feast of the Jews which Jesus attended. Not merely have the modern commentators been perplexed who had to choose between the difficulty of adding one more Passover to the Ministry, or of bringing Jesus to Jerusalem for a visit at some other time of the year, when there seemed nothing in the Synoptic Tradition or in the early belief of the Church to warrant such an extension of the Ministry or such a frequency and variety in our Lord's visits to Jerusalem. Even the earlier Patristic students and the copyists of the sacred text have shown that they were under the spell of the same perplexity. Take the case of the copyists. Probably half the early MSS. have inserted the definite article before "feast," so as to indicate the Passover: "After this was *the* feast of the Jews, and Jesus went up to Jerusalem." That can only mean the Passover. The

---

[1] I have already said something on this point in the pages of the Expositor (December, 1906), but the matter is important and will bear repetition, especially with variations and expansions.

question was discussed as early as the end of the second century, for Irenaeus in counting up how many Passovers Jesus had kept, says that the second Passover was the one at which he healed the paralytic who was lying by the Pool for thirty-eight years.[1] And not a few modern critics have made the same mistakes as Irenaeus about the Passover, as well as continued the curious opinion that the sick man had been waiting thirty-eight years for a successful bath. Another MS. emphasises the belief by adding the words " of unleavened bread." Another inserts the word " their " before the feast, so as to make it the feast of the Jews *par excellence*, just as we find it described in the Peter Gospel.[2] One MS. adds the explanation that it was the Feast of Tabernacles. When we come to the Fathers, we find Chrysostom and Cyril of Alexandria suggesting that it was Pentecost. And what perplexed the ancients did not cease to puzzle

[1] Iren. 147.

[2] The passage in the fragment in Ev Petri is as follows: " And he delivered Him to the people on the day before the Unleavened Bread, which is their Feast."

We should compare the Lewis Syriac in John vi. 4, where we have " Now there was at hand the Feast of the Unleavened Bread of the Jews."

the moderns, who added the Day of Atonement and the Feast of Purim, thus giving us pretty clear demonstration that neither ancients or moderns really knew anything about it. Accordingly Westcott says of the unnamed feast that " it has been identified with each of the three great Jewish Festivals—the *Passover* (Irenaeus, Eusebius, Lightfoot, Neander, Gresswell, &c), *Pentecost* (Cyril, Chrysostom, Calvin, Bengel, &c.), and the *Feast of Tabernacles* (Ewald, &c.). It has also been identified with the *Day of Atonement* (Caspari), the *Feast of Dedication* (Petavius ?), and more commonly in recent times with the *Feast of Purim* (Wieseler, Meyer, Godet, &c.)." That nameless feast has been chased round the calendar as the pool has been hunted round the city. I am now going to explain to you how I was led to a conclusion quite different from these, in spite of the rich variety of choice which they present, at a time when I was not thinking anything about the Gospel of John or our Lord's ministry. It was during the summer of the year 1903 when I was making a journey across Asia Minor from Persia to the Mediterranean, through a region which had been horribly pillaged and devastated by the massacres of 1895 and 1896, and which is still the scene of constant "bleeding white" of the Christian populations. I passed through a village named Habusu, in the plain of Harpoot, and in the course of conversation over the manners and customs of the people, I ascertained that they have a remarkable practice of waiting for the descent of the Angel Gabriel on the night of the New Year. The scene of the descent is supposed to be the village pool, which is dammed up on the previous afternoon in expectation of the event, so as to give more scope to the Angel, and to those who practise the cult. The belief is that the descent of the Angel bestows healing virtues upon the water, and that, in particular, the person who first succeeds in drawing the water after the stroke of midnight will find it turn to gold and silver in his possession. Accordingly the whole population, with the exception of the Protestants, who look upon the business as superstitious, turn out into the water on New Year's eve, in the hope of bettering their fortunes and securing good luck for the coming year.

What struck me at once in this curious custom was the parallel to the account in the Gospel of John, and the first suggestion was that the population of this far inland village between the Taurus ranges, had imitated something which they had read in the Gospel. But there were objections to this. First of all, it was a common custom of both Turks and Christians; second, there was just the variation that one expects in folk-lore practices which have come down out of immemorial antiquity. The Jerusalem custom emphasised health as the blessing brought by the Angel; the Asia Minor practice put the emphasis on wealth and prosperity. Moreover, it was doubtful if the Armenian population could have, at a very early period, such as seems required by the practice of the whole population, transferred the account of the Angel's descent from their Gospel, when it is almost certain that their Gospel did not originally contain the account.

Then I came across the account of a famous Burmese Festival, when the King of the Nats, or Burmese Angels, descends to inaugurate the New Year. It had striking parallels with the Jewish Feast on the one hand, and with the Armeno-Turkish Festival on the other. Here again the festival was timed for midnight on New Year's eve, and the following is the description given of it by Monier Williams:

"When the day arrives, all are on the watch, and just at the right moment, which occurs invariably at midnight, a cannon is fired off announcing the descent of the Nat-King upon earth. Forthwith men and women sally forth out of their houses, carrying pots full of water, consecrated by fresh leaves and twigs of a sacred tree, repeat a formal prayer and pour out the water on the ground. At the same time, all who have guns of any kind discharge them, so as to greet the New Year with as much noise as possible. Then, with the first glimmer of light, all take jars of water and carry them off to the nearest monastery. First they present them to the monks and then proceed to bathe the images." After they have drenched the images of the Buddhas and Bodhisatvas, water throwing becomes universal, and we recognise at once the features of sympathetic magic, and of the rain-charms which are to secure the fertility of the crops in the coming year. Such washing of saints' images, and such throwing about of water (which shows Jupiter Pluvius, or the clerk of the weather, how to do it) are still practised in many parts of Europe.

But what we are concerned with is the parallel

which this affords to the cases already cited. It is quite certain that the Burmese never borrowed their water-festival or their descending angel from Jerusalem or from Armenia. Yet the coincidences are such as to show that, if they did not borrow transversely, they must be deriving the practice vertically from some primeval custom or instinct, whose features can be detected over a very wide area of human life. We may call the festival by the name of "Taking the Luck of the Year" or "Taking the Luck of the Water," for water is the chief feature in the luck of primitive man. Thus we see that in Jerusalem the luck is emphasised as health, in Armenia as wealth, in Burma as fertility and general prosperity. We shall presently be able, I think, to point to traces of this custom within the limits of our own islands. But the first thing that is clear is this, that by the analogy of the Burmese and Armenian customs, the festival in John V. must be a New Year's festival: *it must be the Feast which the Jews call Rosh-ha-Shanah or Head of the Year*: and the Angel must be a part of the machinery of the festival, whether the critics leave him in the text or thrust him out into the margin. As far as I know, the only person who has suspected this is Westcott; and as I sometimes criticise him adversely, I will quote him in full, so as to give his memory due honour, and himself the credit of the discovery. His comment runs as follows:

"It is scarcely likely that the *Day of Atonement* would be called simply a festival . . . but the Feast of Trumpets (the new moon of September) which occurs shortly before, satisfies all the conditions that are required. This 'beginning of the year,' 'the day of memorial' was in every way a most significant day . . . On this day, according to a very early Jewish tradition, God holds a judgment of men (Mishnah, Rosh-ha-Shanah II. and notes): as on this day He created the world. . . . In the ancient prayer attributed to Rav (Second century) which is still used in the synagogue service for the day: 'this day is the day of the beginning of Thy works, a memorial of the first day' . . . And on the provinces it is decreed thereon: 'this one is for the Sword, and this for Peace: this one for Famine and this for Plenty.'" The reference to the Jewish service shows that the New Year's day was one on which the luck was fixed: more exactly, I suspect, it was in debate, and was finally fixed by God and the Angels ten days after on the Day of Atonement.[1]

So then the scene in John V. is to be laid on some September evening (for the day begins at sundown, and the New Year); the people are waiting for the trumpets to sound the New Year (the trumpets answering to the guns in the Burmese Festival), and while they are waiting Jesus passes by and observes a man who is hoping to get the Luck of the Water. We are not to assume that the man had been waiting long at the Pool, say for thirty-eight years, as some have suggested. The language of the Gospel is quite clear: "Jesus knew that he has been sick long by now, γνοὺς ὅτι πολὺν χρόνον ἔχει" which corresponds exactly to the words that precede, " he has passed thirty-eight years in this malady of his " (τριάκοντα καὶ ὄκτω ἔτη ἔχων ἐν τῇ ἀσθενείᾳ αὐτοῦ).

But there is, I suggest, a probability that they

---

[1] For instance, the Mishna says that at the Feast of Tabernacles, the Water question is decided for the Year. Hence there used to be a Water-libation on that Festival, which may be interpreted as a prayer for rain. Rabbi Simeon ben Jochai taught that if Israel were found worthy at the moment of the New Year they would receive abundance of rain; but if unworthy the rain would be dispersed over seas, rivers, &c.

tried the Luck of the Year in Jerusalem every day from the new moon up to the Day of Atonement. If that were so, it would explain every detail in the story, including a possible repeated failure to get the "Luck." Moreover the new explanation would restore historical value to a story in John which, up to the present, has appeared increasingly suspicious. When we get the geography and the calendar indication right, and the folk-lore of the time right, we may fairly contend that we are interpreting history and not merely piously playing with legends. Nor does the central figure of the incident lose any dignity when He appears in the midst of a people practising an ancient cult, and without stopping to discuss their cult, tells the man who is looking for aid from that unsatisfying quarter, to take up his mat and go home. He would doubtless say the same if He were to appear amongst the pilgrims at Lourdes, who really represent an unconscious survival of the same practices as used to prevail throughout so wide an area of human life. "If Christ came to Lourdes,"—well, He would do the same as when he came to Bethesda.

But you will ask me before leaving this part

of the subject and giving you some concluding touches from the region of folk-lore, to tell you something about that disputed verse, which records the descent of the Angel. Dr. Burgon, too, and Dr. Hort will both want to know what I am going to say on the question of the text. For instance Dr. Burgon tells us (p. 283) "The troubling of the Pool of Bethesda is not even allowed a bracketed place in Dr. Hort's Text. How the accomplished critic would have set about persuading the Anti-Nicene Fathers that they were in error for holding it to be genuine Scripture, it is hard to imagine." (p. 311), "The words which he insists on thrusting out of the Text are often conspicuous *for the very quality* which (by the hypothesis) was the warrant for their exclusion:" i.e., they have the ring of genuineness which Dr. Hort denies them. I think it must be concluded that our enquiry has not diminished the ring of genuineness about the famous descent of the Angel. At the same time it seems impossible to regard it as a part of the primitive text. On the other hand, if not a part of the primitive text, it must be very early, for two reasons; first of all, it has coloured almost the whole of the Western Latin tradition;

second, if added, it must be a Palestinian addition, for who else but one who was closely acquainted with Jerusalem customs could have added the explanation. Moreover the writer of the explanation knows that it is an annual custom for the Angel to descend at a particular feast, and says so. So we find ourselves again in agreement with Westcott who says that the disputed words "form a very early note added to explain v. 7 [i.e. the troubling of the water], *while the Jewish tradition with regard to the Pool was still fresh.*" Well, if the words were added when the Gospels were still under Palestine influence and emendation, we must be at a very early period. And I think the gloss should stand on the margin or in a foot-note, both on account of its antiquity and because of its furnishing the correct explanation of what took place. But I am afraid this would hardly satisfy Dean Burgon's *manes*, any more than I could satisfy him if I said I would accept *Bethedsa* in place of *Bethesda*. I did not expect when I took up the loose threads of this investigation to find that the enquiry would go so far to endorse his protest against the marginal readings, "Why encumber yourself with such a note at all?" Certainly for English readers there does not seem the least necessity to change the conventional Bethesda.

And now for a few concluding remarks on *the Luck of the Water* and *the Luck of the New Year*. Did they take the luck in these islands? Here are some considerations which suggest that they did. Here is an extract from a letter in the Transactions of the *Woolhope* [Hereford] *Naturalists' Field Club* for 1898—1899.

"THE LUCK OF THE YEAR."

" There is a custom that I have heard of in North Herefordshire, and I have acquaintance with those that have seen it: it is practised on New Year's Day and the 'Luck of the Year' is supposed to depend upon it. It is considered an omen of bad luck if a girl or woman be the first to come from the outside into the house. It is therefore devoutly desired that the first to cross the threshold should be a member of the male sex. Should this be so the visitor is invited to drink of the 'Dew of the Well,' i.e., to be the first to draw and to drink water from the well. After this is accomplished the visitor returns to the house and is invited to be the first in the

The Verdict of Succeeding Days. 65

New Year to draw cider and to partake of cake with the newly-drawn cider. Upon leaving he is given a coin." Here we have the Luck coming in the form of a person, or rather the Luck of the First Foot, but the point I want you to notice is that he is the first to drink of the water of the well in the New Year. That is where he gets his Luck from. It is exactly parallel to the Armenian belief that prosperity will follow the first person who gets the water consecrated by the descending angel.[1]

Here is another interesting testimony from Herefordshire which is even clearer.[2]

"At Bromyard[3] and its neighbourhood, as

---

[1] For the "Luck of the First-foot," cf John v. 4 ("Whosoever first steppeth in,") and note that in the North of England "the first-foot across the threshold is watched with great anxiety," the good or bad luck of the house during the year depending on the first comer being a man or a woman.
Notes and Queries, 2nd ser. vol. xi. p. 244.

[2] For these points I am indebted to Thiselton Dyer's *British Popular Customs, Past and Present*, 1876.

[3] I am especially interested in Bromyard, because it is an outlying centre of the worship of a Midland deity. To explain what I mean: most persons are aware from Mr. Kipling's Puck of Pook's Hill that the spirit whom we call Puck was once honoured in Sussex by our forefathers.

twelve o'clock on the 31st of December draws near the last of the Christmas carols are heard without doors, and a pleasurable excitement is playing on the faces of the family around the last Christmas log within, a rush is made to the nearest spring of water, and whoever is fortunate *to first bring in the* '*cream of the well*,' as it is termed, and those who first taste of it, have ' prospect of good luck through the forthcoming year.' "—*The Antiquary*, 1873, Vol. iii. p. 7.

Have they noticed him in Hertfordshire at Puckeridge, and just outside Bournemouth at Pokesdown? There is something similar to this in the place-names of the Midlands. I am writing in Birmingham or Bromwich-ham, to the north of me there is West Bromwich and Little Bromwich, and Bromford Bridge (the Bridge being a later addition to the original ford); then to the S.W. there is Bromsgrove (originally Bromesgrave), which suggests at once the cult of a deity, and over in Hereford there are Bromyard and Bromfield which convey nearly the same impression. When the people in these parts abbreviate Birmingham, they call it Brum, and I suspect that Brum or Brom was the original tribal deity of this district. Was he the Thunder-God (cf. Βρέμω, fremo), or must we look for some other explanation? Perhaps Miss Harrison, who knows all about the worship of Bromios, will tell us (see *Proleg. to Study of Greek Religion* p. 414), I am loth, for the sake of the people amongst whom I dwell, to accept her explanation that Bromios means Beer-God. I shall, perhaps, try to show presently that it is the Celtic deity Bormo.

There is a similar custom reported from the South of Scotland. In the South of Scotland, as soon as the clock has struck the midnight hour, one of a family goes to the well as quickly as possible and carefully skims it: this they call getting the scum or ream of the well.

'Twall struck—twa neighbour hizzies raise,
  An liltin' gaed a sad gate,
The flower of the well to our house gaes
  An' I'll the bonniest lad get'.

The "*flower of the well*" signifies the first pail of water, and the girl who is so fortunate as to obtain the prize is supposed to have more than a double chance of obtaining the most accomplished young man in the parish.—*Med. aevi Kalend.*, Vol. i., p. 129.

Here a race for the Luck seems to be implied, and we are very near to the "Whosoever first," &c., of the Gospel. The parallelism between the "flower of the well" in the Lowlands and the "cream of the well," &c., in Herefordshire, will be noticed. Clearly we are in the same cycle of beliefs and practices.

Further North the New Year's water drawing takes a more solemn form, there seems to be no race for it, and it is used for aspersion as in the Burmese festival. Here is an account of it: "As soon as the last night of the year sets in, it is the signal with the Strathdown Highlander for the suspension of his usual employment, and he directs his attention to more agreeable callings. The men form into bands with axes, and shaping their course to the juniper bushes, they return home laden with mighty loads, which are arranged round the fire to dry until morning. A certain discreet person is dispatched to the 'dead and living ford' to draw a pitcher of water in profound silence, without the vessel touching the ground, lest its virtue should be destroyed, and on his return all retire to rest. Early on New Year's morning the *Usquecashrichd*, or water from the *dead and living ford* is drunk, as a potent charm until next New Year's day, against the spells of witchcraft, the malignity of evil eyes, and the activity of all infernal agency. The qualified Highlander then takes a large brush, with which he profusely asperses the occupants of all beds; from whom it is not unusual for him to receive ungrateful remonstrances against ablution." [Then follows the purification of the house with smoke from the juniper bushes.] *Popular Superstitions of the Highlanders of Scotland.* Stewart, 1851.

Here we again recognise that the Luck of the New Year is the Luck of the Water. There is also the sense that one may draw either Water of Life or Water of Death, and that great care must be taken to have the right person to secure the Luck: so here again we are on the track of the same old customs.

I have said enough to show how widely these customs are spread. One touch of folk-lore makes the whole world kin. And there is no irreverence in proving the existence of folk-lore in Palestine, or pointing to traces of it in the New Testament. It becomes really valuable if it vindicates the historical character of certain sections in the fourth Gospel.

APPENDIX TO LECTURE II.

Since writing this lecture I have had the happiness of reading Dr. G. A. Smith's great book on Jerusalem, and finding myself in cordial disagreement with it on certain points, and in particular, on his treatment of Bethesda. I will take up the principal points *seriatim* so that the ground may be clear for further discussion, and note both where we agree and where we differ, as actual students of the topography of the Holy City.

1. We agree with one another in the following statement with the exception of the last clause:—

Vol. i., p. 118. "North of this [i.e. the Birket Isra'il] and on the west side of the Church of St. Anne, beneath vaults on which rest the remains of probably two churches, is a pool cut out of the rock on at least two sides, 55 feet long and $12\frac{1}{2}$ broad (almost 17 metres by 3.8) with another beside it.[1] No trace of a spring has

[1] P.E.F.Q. 1888. 117 ff.
Z.D.P.V. xi. 178 ff.

been found or an aqueduct: the water, which gathers sometimes to the depth of 20 feet, is immediately drawn from the surface. There can be no doubt that we have here the twin pools which, from the time of Eusebius at least till the end of the sixth century, were identified with the pool of Bethesda; but from that to the pool actually intended by St. John is, as we shall find, a far cry indeed." All right as we shall find, except the last clause. Note the admission that the pools at St. Anne's are identified from the time of Eusebius with Bethesda: these are then the pools of the Bordeaux pilgrim.

2. We are agreed that this quarter of the city is called Bezetha, but we are not agreed what is the interpretation. I will collect what G.A.S. says on the subject.

i. p. 18, note 4. "Bezetha may equal Beth-zaith, *House of Olives*. So Dr. Hort and the Codex Sinaiticus; the Syriac N.T., calls the Mount of Olives *Beth-zaithe*." No doubt about the etymology of Beth-zatha. But the question is as to the equation between Bezatha and Beth-zatha.

ii. p. 244, note 2. After quoting Josephus'

account of the position of Bezetha relatively to the Tower of Antonia, the note adds to the text: B.J. iv. 2. "I have omitted the strange meaning which Josephus gives to the name Bezetha: 'this recently built quarter is called in the vernacular Bezetha, which, if interpreted in the Greek tongue, would be called New-City.' More correctly in ii. B.J. xix. 4, Josephus says that Bezetha (here in Niese's text spelt Betheza) was *also* called New-City. Bezetha cannot mean New-City: probably it stands for Beth-zaith, 'house' or 'district of Olives.'"

Here the attempt is made to suggest that New-town is an alternative name, the suggestion is absolutely negatived by the previous passage which G.A.S. has quoted ('ἐκλήθη δ' ἐπιχωρίως Βεζεθά τὸ νεόκτιστον μέρος, ὃ μεθερμηνευόμενον 'ελλάδι γλώσσῃ, καινὴ λέγοιτ' ἂν πόλις.

Here it is said distinctly that Βεζεθά may be translated as *New-town*. Moreover G. A. Smith omits to notice the significance of Niese's change of the text to *Betheza* (for *Betheza* is phonetically the same as *Bethedsa*). No case is, therefore, made out for contradicting Josephus' etymology or for replacing Betheza (Bezetha) by Bethzatha.

Appendix to Lecture II. 73

3. In Vol. ii. p. 564 ff, is a definite discussion of the site of Bethesda. First the problem is discussed textually, the three contending readings being compared: Bethesda, Bethzatha and Bethsaida. (Some of the references are wrong: L is quoted for Βηθζαθά, and a reference is made to a certain Codex at Leiden without saying what it is a MS. of.)[1] We then have the statement as to the meaning of the names that none of them is clear. Bethesda as *house of mercy* is not certain: Bethzatha was the name of the quarter of the city to the North of the Temple. Bethsaida, " house of hunting " or " of fishing," though well supported is hardly appropriate to Jerusalem, and may easily have arisen to an error of the ear for Bethzaitha, " place of Olives," or by confusion with the Galilean place name. Here we have a question raised as to whether Bethesda could mean *House of Mercy*: if it couldn't why did the Syriac translators write it Beth-ḥesda and

---

[1] Apparently this is taken from Encyc Bibl s.v. Bethesda which begins " Bethesda (ΒΗΘΕΣΔΑ) cod. leid. . . . i.e. House of Mercy." Here again there seems no clue by which to identify the Codex Leidensis or its readings. What is it? A MS. of the Greek N.T. or the Peshito or the Onomasticon? Certainly the last, but it should not be quoted, for it is wrong.

the Arabic Tatian write Betharrahmat? And why did the pious people place the Church of St. Anne in the neighbourhood, because of the similarity between Bethesda and Beit-Hanna, each of which means House of Grace? See Clermont Ganneau, quoted by G.A.S. in Vol. ii. p. 566, or why should Josephus (B.J. V. 474) say that a certain man from Adiabene was called Ἀγίρας, which signifies "lame," unless he is transliterating the Syriac ḥagir?[1]

Here again we have the false equation between Bezetha and Bethzatha which has now crept from the notes into the text, so that the quarter of the city is now Bethzatha which is certainly not Josephus' form. The judgment about the improbability of Bethsaida is correct, but Sanday is quoted rightly in a note as saying that "the combination of two authorities so wide apart as

---

[1] Notice too how he oscillates in the spelling of Hebron between Ἐβρών and Χεβρών, and in Hilkiah between Ἐλκίας and Χελκίας; and what about Ἐνώχ for Hanokh? or Θαβὼρ καὶ Ἑρμών in Ps. lxxxviii. 13. And how should we expect the name of Hezekiah to be written in Greek? Will not Ἐζεκίας do? Must it be Χισκίας? Can G. A. S. be right in saying that it is doubtful whether an original ḥi or ḥe would be represented in Greek by ε?

Appendix to Lecture II. 75

Tertullian and B. carries the reading back to a remote antiquity."[1]

But then, as Burgon would say, "Have you not yet found out, Sir, that all various readings are early?"

The good point made in the textual enquiry is the recognition that the name of the pool and the name of the quarter of the city, are the same. But the name itself is wrong. And now we come to an extraordinary statement which we quote in full:

ii. p. 566. "At least six sites have been proposed: The Hammam esh-Shefâ, the Twin-pools adjoining the North-West corner of Antonia, the Birket Israin, the Twin-pools at St. Anne's, the Virgin's Well or Gihon, and Siloam. Tradition supports in succession the second, third and fourth of these. The Twin-pools by Antonia are probably those identified with Bethesda by the Bordeaux pilgrim, Eucherius, Eusebius and Jerome; the Birkit Israin has been connected with our passage since the thirteenth

---

[1] Only Sanday doesn't remind us that when we push the reading back on the faith of Tertullian we are pushing back the angel as well, for Tertullian says (piscinam Bethsaidam angelus interveniens commovebat, *De Bapt.* 5).

century; and the pools of St. Anne's at least since the Crusades." Compare this statement with the one quoted above in which it is definitely conceded that "there can be no doubt that we have here [at St. Anne's] the twin-pools which from the time of Eusebius at least to the end of the sixth century, were identified with the Pool of Bethesda." It is a far cry from the Crusades to the beginning of the fourth century. After having got rid of the pools at St. Anne's by contradicting his own statements and making their identification a matter of the Middle Ages, it was comparatively easy to wander off to the Virgin's Spring and conclude that "the balance of evidence therefore is in favour of the Virgin's Spring, but the whole is uncertain."

But if the Virgin's Spring is the real pool, what becomes of the identification of the name of the pool with the name of the N.E. corner of the city; an identification which still stands in the text? The Virgin's Pool is not in Bezetha, and it could not, for certain, be described as a "place of olives." That name must belong to an area, not to a hole.

We are obliged to conclude, then, that G. A. Smith has got into confusion, through the conflicting character of the evidence involved or by writing passages over again after a lapse of time without due caution. I hope the matter is now reasonably clear.

FOLK-LORE OF SUNDERLAND AND DISTRICT (N.E. DURHAM).

FIRST-FOOTING.

The following note on the first-foot and the New Year in the North of England was given me by one of my students: the Luck of the Water appears to have disappeared and to be replaced or continued by the Luck of the First-foot.

"A custom known as *first-footing* is practised by almost *the whole* of the population. It consists of the following ceremony, which has only very slight variations among the different classes.

(1) A man (*never in any case a woman*) is chosen to be 'first-foot'; some people have a preference for *dark* complexioned men and some for those with *light* complexions; whilst some prefer blue eyes and some brown; others choose old men, but some will have only young men (I

myself was 'first-foot' at the age of twelve).

(2) The person chosen always leaves the house before 12.0 p.m. on New Year's eve, and by some means obtains (in *no* case from the house where he is going to be "first-foot") a piece of coal, some bread or other food, and anything else he cares to procure. Then as soon as 12.0 p.m. has passed and the New Year dawns he enters the house and gives the coal and food to the first person he comes in contact with. There is much hand-shaking and well-wishing, and when this is over the first-foot must partake of refreshment in the shape of wine, tea, spirits, or some other liquid; he must also cut the New Year's cake, and be the first to partake of it. After this is over, all and sundry are welcome to enter and an 'open' house is kept the whole night through."

Another of my students writes me at the New Year, from Belfast, that she has just been round, according to promise, to cross the threshold of a superstitious old lady, who likes to have a dark person in first; and that she had taken a little wreath of straw for her to hang up to make the ritual quite complete.

LECTURE III.

Some Speculations of Textual Criticism Justified.

IN our previous Lecture we were discussing some points in connexion with the famous story of the Troubling of the Pool by the Angel; and we were able to explain the incident without any fanciful references to intermittent springs or rock-syphons or possible medicinal qualities of the water, by transporting ourselves into the region of folk-lore and studying elsewhere than in Palestine, and unencumbered by the traditions of pious commentators, phenomena which are similar to those recorded in the fifth chapter of John. Incidentally we discussed outside the region of Textual Criticism, what was the real name of the pool, and what its position; and we were able to arrive at satisfactory conclusions for both; and we showed that the alternative readings proposed for the name of the pool in the Revised Version were both of them incorrect, and that the real name was much nearer to that which the modern critics expel from the text. The result was new and to some extent surprising. It vindicated at all events Dr. Burgon's protest against the encumbrance of the margin with notes as to readings which cannot be correct.

Now I do not really suppose that Burgon cared very much whether the famous pool was called Bethesda or Bethedsa [Betheza]: he certainly would not have torn up the trees in his

"Vast Typhoean rage more fell"

over a little innocent question about the spelling of the name of a pond. He was far more concerned over the complete extrusion of the account of the Angel that troubled the waters: he had lost a supernatural being. He had been shorn of a miracle; both the miracle and the miracle-worker were attested by Catholic Tradition; therefore they must stay within the covers and compass of the sacred text. If the oldest MSS. leave them out, so much the worse for the oldest MSS. Outside the Catholic Church and its imagined unity, all men and all MSS. are liars.

Speculations of Textual Criticism Justified. 81

Most people would have been thankful that Textual Criticism had relieved them of the burden of that periodic angel, who haunted a certain patch of dirty water in Jerusalem. We have, ourselves, at times, indulged in that form of inward congratulation, just as we are thankful that one can believe in the Gospel of Mark without being committed to the thaumaturgy of the last twelve verses. But with Dean Burgon the excisions made in the text stood together: he resented them all: and he hated those who made them. I hope I have shown that there is a ground of reconciliation between those who love the story of the Angel and those who have no sympathy with it; and that both sides may unite on a folk-lore basis in concluding "the thing never really happened," but " what really happened was that people thought it did." And as I said, the supposed gloss is certainly entitled to a marginal place in Greek Testaments and in English Translations. I hope this will satisfy the shades of the great dead, as well as the Angel Gabriel who is the principal sufferer by the criticism.

But now I want to say a few words about the general effect of the excision of passages from the New Testament on the ground that they are not found in the oldest MSS., or do not appear to belong to the books in which they are found. This is probably the most portentous feature about the newer dissection of the Gospels; they appear to have been put together piecemeal. The knife is applied to a crack here, or a seam there, and a whole section comes away. A breach of continuity is detected: then some chapters must have been misplaced, or some intervening matter does not properly belong there. The changes occur often at the most vital points in the narrative; the Prayer upon the Cross goes: the words of Institution are lost from the Lord's Supper; the story of the adulteress to whom our Lord spoke words of authoritative mercy are relegated to an appendix. Whole sections appear decorated with brackets and stars, implying that they are strangers and foreigners in the places where we find them. One would not mind so much if it had only been the verses in Matthew about the Signs of the Sky and the Signs of the Times, or the statement that "Old wine is a better drink than new wine"; but when we come to the mutilation of the Lord's Prayer or the excision of the Agony in the Garden, surely Dean Burgon might say,

Speculations of Textual Criticism Justified. 83

"I do well to be angry." At all events he would have done well to be angry (within limits) if his anger had followed his intelligence, and if the verdict of his judgment had been countersigned by the discoveries and investigations of the "succeeding days" to which he made his final appeal, as he said, with serene confidence. Unfortunately, as we shall see, the verdict of "Time that trieth Truth" appears to be often against him.

In Dr. Hort's presentation of the N.T. text, the pages are frequently disfigured by double brackets, implying a residual uncertainty as to what is contained within them. These commonly mean that, in the judgment of the editors the words affected are not a part of the original text. One would have supposed that in that case such words would have been promptly removed to the foot-notes or the appendix. But apparently the courage of the editors failed at the last moment, and they express themselves, through Dr. Hort, as follows:

"None can feel more strongly than ourselves that it might at first sight appear the duty of faithful critics to remove completely from the text any words or passages which they believe not to have originally formed part of the work in which they occur. But there are circumstances connected with the text of the New Testament which have withheld us from adopting this obvious mode of proceeding."

On examining the circumstances, to which Dr. Hort alludes, it appears that while they believed the passages in question not to be a part of the text, they did not feel quite sure that they did so believe. So they consecrated their vacillation by the use of double brackets, but expressed themselves, as a rule, quite positively on the matter in the appendix. And this hesitation has led to one curious result in an opposite direction. In Matthew xxvii. 49 quite a number of ancient authorities, including the Vatican and Sinai MSS., insert a statement that "another with a spear pierced His side and there came out blood and water." The language agrees closely with the corresponding statement in John, but the doctrine differs: in Matthew His wound is inflicted before death, in John after death, and to establish the fact that He was dead. In spite of this change in the point of view, most scholars will find it very hard to believe that it is anything but a transfer from the text of John, probably by way of a Harmony of the Passion

Gospels. But the sentence is so well attested in Matthew by the authorities whom Westcott and Hort always follow that they put it into the text as if it belonged there, and then marked it for removal, as if it did not belong there.

But now we are in danger of getting into the jungle of the various readings, from which I wanted to keep you clear. Let me keep to my main question, the verdict of time with regard to the excisions made in the text by the critics. I will take three notable cases, in each of which there seems to have come some fresh evidence to hand since the publication of the Revised Version. The evidence which I am to present relates to the authorship of the passages impugned. And after all, if we could get at it, that is the real point which we want to know. Dr. Hort's method of summing up the question of authorship usually consists in saying that it is " a singular interpolation, evidently from an extraneous source, written or oral." " The influence[1] of extraneous records or traditions of one kind or another is clearly perceptible in some cases and its presence may with more or less probability be suspected in others." If that is a correct judgment, we

[1] Introd. p. 296.

ought surely to be able, sometimes, to unearth some of the written records to which allusion is made, or to come across traces of their authors. Is it likely that investigation should be wholly barren into the origin of the materials, which, according to Dr. Hort, were so freely incorporated by the pious scribes of the second century? We will take three cases, as I said, and examine the results of modern enquiry as to their authorship. The first shall be the last twelve verses of St. Mark: the second shall be the Prayer of our Lord upon the Cross: the third (which we will treat very briefly) shall be the story of the adulteress.

1. The last twelve verses of St. Mark were the subject of Dr. Burgon's great monograph, in which he assailed those who were for removing these verses from the text, and, as he believed, smote his antagonists hip and thigh with a great slaughter. It is not necessary for me to go in detail into the objections that have been made against the authenticity of these verses. We are probably familiar with the main points of the indictment: their absence from the oldest texts of the New Testament, the existence of an alternative ending of a highly rhetorical

character which no one can believe to be by the hand of Mark; the abrupt return of the narrative in the ordinary text to an earlier point of the narration, intimating that a fresh Resurrection account is being used; and the internal evidence of this new Resurrection account against its Marcan authorship: all of these things are sufficiently known now to English readers. We are aware now that the Gospel is shorn of its last twelve verses, and ends abruptly with the words " And they were afraid—" which is not a literary ending, nor a Christian ending, and can hardly be a Greek ending:[1] so that we are obliged to assume that the real ending of Mark is gone, and speculate as we please as to what has become of it and what it was like. Some persons who have a certain amount of imagination will say that the last leaf was absent from an early copy, others that it is substantially

[1] It was simply the accepted conclusion of the Gospel for a certain space of its history. The remarkable confirmation of this by Mrs. Lewis's Syriac Gospels from Mount Sinai is now well known. It was an interesting moment when the brush dipped in re-agent brought up the missing colophon to the Gospel, and showed that the oldest Syriac Gospel was on the side of the two oldest Greek uncials in stopping short with "they were afraid," and adding no alternative.

preserved in the end of Matthew or in the last chapter of John: others that Mark was interrupted just as he was finishing or that he had to catch a train or something of the kind, and never got back to his desk again. I am not going to speculate on these matters, further than to tell you the first two words that will be found on the missing leaf, if it should ever be recovered. The narrative went on like this: [For they were afraid] of the Jews:

ἐφοβοῦντο γὰρ τοὺς Ἰουδαίους.

But I am anticipating matters by taking sides, and assuming that the last twelve verses are not genuine. Let us hold our hand and see what has happened with regard to the end of Mark. The most recent thing is the discovery of a new and expanded ending to the Gospel. Early in 1907 a number of ancient manuscripts were on sale in Cairo by a dealer named Ali Arabi. They comprised fourth and fifth century copies or portions of the Old and New Testaments in Greek, and were said to have come from the town of Akhmîm (the ancient Panopolis), a place which will be remembered by the recovery from one of its tombs of portions of the Book of Enoch and the Gospel and Revelation of Peter in 1886.

The MSS. in question were examined by Messrs. Grenfell and Hunt and offered to the British Museum, which for some reason or other that I am not able to divine declined to buy them. So they passed to America, and became the property of Mr. Freer, of Detroit, who has placed them for publication in the hands of one of the professors of the Michigan University. I may say in passing that the assumption that the MSS. were obtained by excavation at Akhmîm is an illusion: they came from a famous Coptic Monastery, and another batch from the same haul have gone to Berlin. When the Freer MSS. came to be examined, it was found that the text of the last verses of Mark (contained in one of the precious codices, written perhaps in the fifth century) was accompanied by notable expansion. It ran on in normal fashion till the end of the 14th verse, and then proceeded something like this:

"And they defended themselves saying that this age of lawlessness and sin is under the power of Satan, who, through unclean spirits, does not suffer the true virtue of God to be apprehended. Therefore now reveal Thy righteousness. And Christ addressed them and said, 'The limit of the years of the authority of Satan has been reached, but other dread things are coming: and it was for those who had sinned that I was delivered to death that they might return to the Truth and sin no more, but inherit the spiritual and immortal glory of righteousness in heaven, but go ye into all the world, &c.,'" and then the Gospel concludes conventionally. Of this extraordinary expansion no Greek trace has been preserved, but Jerome had given a translation of the first lines of the expansion and said that he had found it in Greek MSS. So here we had the problem of the last verses of Mark accentuated by another very striking piece of material, belonging apparently to a very early period.

We may be quite sure that this is not the lost ending of Mark. It corresponds in literary style with the short ending which Westcott and Hort print as an alternative for the last twelve verses: I mean the passage which tells us that "All that mean the passage which tells us that " All that had been enjoined to them they reported to Peter and his company. And after this also Jesus Himself [appeared to them] and from the East to the West sent forth by their means the holy and immortal preaching of the eternal Gospel." The new expansion is fitted on to the last twelve

Speculations of Textual Criticism Justified. 91

verses and so, I suppose, ought not to be used in evidence against them: but it is certainly in evidence for the freedom with which the close of Mark was being handled, and this laxity in dealing with the text implies that something had gone wrong with the conclusion of Mark from the beginning and the scribes were aware of the fact. So we have one more important piece of evidence as to the unsettlement of the text. But there is no sign of authorship, although we may be quite sure the style is not that of Mark. And, as we have said, even if we push this new section back into early times, we are driving the last twelve verses of Mark before it.

But who really doubts the antiquity of the last twelve verses of Mark? Surely that point might be freely conceded: though I remember once having a battle with my friend, the late Dr. Moulton, over it, when he protested vigorously against something which I had said to that effect. I believe he thought I was Burgonizing: but I think he was quite convinced by my statements that the antiquity of the last twelve verses had been underestimated. And if any one had any doubt upon it, the discovery of the actual authorship to which I am now going to refer, will be decisive on the point. Many of you will remember the discovery made by Mr. F. C. Conybeare of an ancient Armenian MS. in the convent at Edschmiazin, in Russian Armenia, which had the last twelve verses of Mark actually spaced off from the rest of the Gospel, and in the intervening space a line was written in red, containing the words:

Ariston Eridzou

i.e. of Ariston the Presbyter.

So here at last was the missing evidence for the authorship of the last twelve verses, and a discovery for critical confirmation which should be the end of all strife. The only remaining question would appear to be as to the exact person intended. Two suggestions arose at once to the mind of scholars: either that it was Aristo of Pella, who in the reign of Hadrian wrote an account of a disputation between a Jew and a Christian relating to the Old Testament predictions of Christ: or else it must be the Aristion who is mentioned along with the Presbyter John in a famous passage from the second century, in which Papias records how he had been in the habit of collecting traditions from those who had been hearers of the Apostles, with a view to finding out from them what Andrew or Peter had said, or what Philip or Thomas or James or John or Matthew or any other of the Lord's disciples, or what Aristion and the Presbyter John, the disciples of the Lord, say. The suggestion, then, at once arises that this Aristion whom Papias recorded as a walking repository of traditions of the Lord, a real live index-man, is the person to whom the Armenian MS. refers. Papias does not actually call him a Presbyter; but as he couples him with a John who is called the Presbyter John, when he comes to distinguish him from the Apostle John, it may reasonably be imagined that Presbyter is also his ecclesiastical appellation. So I think we may say that the author of the last twelve verses is found, and that the verdict of time inclines strongly against the Burgon contentions. There does not seem to be much room for hesitation: but a cautious judgment would perhaps be that of Dr. Swete, in his *Introduction to the Gospel of Mark* (p. cxiii).

"The documentary evidence for the longer ending is, as we have seen, overwhelming. Nevertheless there are points at which the chain of evidence is not merely weak but broken.

Besides the fact that in the fourth century, if not in the third, the 'accurate copies' of the Gospel were known to end with XVI. 8, and that in the two great fourth century Bibles which have come down to us the Gospel actually ends at this point, those who maintain the genuineness of the last twelve verses have to account for the early circulation of an alternative ending, and for the ominous silence of the Ante-Nicene fathers between Irenaeus and Eusebius in reference to a passage which was of so much importance both on historical and theological ground. When we add to these defects in the external evidence the internal characteristics which distinguish these verses from the rest of the Gospel it is impossible to resist the conclusion that they belong to another work, whether that of Aristion or some unknown writer of the first century." So Dr. Swete, with excess of caution: for surely if we have a conviction that the longer ending is due to a writer of the time of Aristion, and if we turn up an early piece of direct evidence which says it was Aristion, there does not seem much excuse for hesitation.[1]

---

[1] Professor Burkitt expresses the following obscure verdict in Encyc. Bibl. Vol. 4, Col. 5011 (*Texts and Versions*).

Speculations of Textual Criticism Justified. 95

The evidence has, however, been vigorously resisted in one or two quarters. Schmiedel in the *Encyclopedia Biblica* (*Resurrection Narratives*, col. 4050) tries to show that as there is nothing new in the summary which we call the last twelve verses, it cannot be by Aristion; " There is no particular reason why we should assign to a personal disciple of Jesus such as Aristion the authorship of so meagre an excerpt as Mark xvi. 9-20 from which absolutely nothing new is to be learned." But we may have to allow some latitude in the interpretation of discipleship, and there is a suspicion that the summary was introduced in order to avoid saying things which should contradict the other evangelists: hence meagreness is in order.

Professor Bacon, of Yale University, has developed a marvellous theory to account for the heading " of Ariston the Presbyter." According to him the Armenian scribe who made it had

---

"The inference is that the scribe of the MS. or of its archetype, had access to a tradition that Aristion, the friend of Papias . . . was the man who added the verses at the end of the second Gospel. This would seem to be fifty years too early if other indications are to be trusted." The passage is not clear. Fifty years too early for what? And who said that Aristion added the verses?

been reading the History of Moses of Chorene, and understood Moses to say that Hadrian made Aristo of Pella the secretary of Mark when he appointed him (Marcus) Bishop of Jerusalem. And hence he attributes the appendix to the Elder Aristo, the secretary of Mark. It must be allowed that this is a very learned scribe and Professor Bacon a very ingenious person to have discovered him. Everybody misunderstands everything. Mark the Evangelist becomes Marcus the Bishop of Jerusalem in the second century: Aristo of Pella is imagined to have been his secretary, and is therefore imagined to have finished the book which Marcus did not write. One may prove anything by dealing with documentary evidence in this way, and the laws of probability may be finally abolished. But as I do not suppose any one has been seriously affected by these conjectures, I do not need to go further after them into the wilderness.[1]

2. We will now take the second passage to which I referred: the Prayer of our Lord upon the Cross as recorded in Luke xxiii. 34. No one will

---

[1] Bacon's statement will be found under the heading "Aristion" in Hastings' *Dictionary of Christ and the Gospels*. There is a further reference on the subject in *Journal of Bibl. Lit.* for 1908, pp. 1—23.

Speculations of Textual Criticism Justified. 97

like to see these words shut up in double brackets, as though they were doubtful, because we have an irresistible conviction that the passage could never have been invented; and there is perhaps no change in the whole of the Gospels which produced such an outburst of feeling on the part of Dr. Burgon. I must quote you a passage to show what I mean. "These twelve precious words: ('Then said Jesus, Father, forgive them; for they know not what they do'), Drs. Westcott and Hort enclose within double brackets in token of the 'moral certainty' they entertain that the words are spurious. And yet these words are found in every *known uncial* and in *every known cursive copy*, except four; besides being found in *every ancient Version*: and *what*,—(we ask the question with sincere simplicity),—what amount of evidence is calculated to inspire undoubting confidence in any existing Reading, if not such a concurrence of authorities as this? . . . We forbear to insist upon the probabilities of the case. The divine power and sweetness of the incident shall not be enlarged upon. We introduce no considerations resulting from Internal Evidence. True, that 'few verses of the Gospels bear in themselves a surer witness to the Truth of what they record, than this.' (It is the admission of the very man who has nevertheless dared to brand it with suspicion.) But we reject his loathsome patronage with indignation. ' Internal Evidence '—' Transcriptional Probability,' and all such ' chaff and draff ' with which he fills his pages *ad nauseam*, and mystifies nobody but himself—shall be allowed no place in the present discussion."[1] Burgon then proceeds to collect more than forty Patristic witnesses to the verse, and it is evident that he is as learned as he is angry."

Meanwhile Dr. Hort, on the other side, maintained that it had come into the Gospel of Luke from an extraneous source, and showed that the evidence against it was very strong. It seems clear that it was unknown to the oldest forms of the Latin and Egyptian Versions, in spite of Burgon's claim to all the versions. Since then the discovery of the Lewis Syriac shows that it was originally absent from the Syriac Version, so that all three of the great versions (Latin, Egyptian and Syriac) began without it. There were other weak spots in the champion's armour: but still the question must arise as to the possible source of such a tradition.

[1] *Revision Revised*, pp. 82, 83.

Speculations of Textual Criticism Justified. 99

Who else could have recorded it? Should we not have the extraneous record attested by someone if it had really existed? Now at this point I want to give a curious piece of evidence which has lately come to light. There is a late Latin writer whose works are preserved in the Patrology of the name of Haymo. He was Bishop of Halberstadt in the first half of the ninth century, and had studied in his early days in the famous monastery at Fulda, under Rabanus Maurus. Amongst the many commentaries which he wrote upon the Scripture both of the Old and New Testaments, there is one on Isaiah, and if we turn to his comments upon Isaiah LIII. we shall find the following remarkable statement:[1] " Pro transgressoribus Judaeis sive persecutoribus rogavit dicens dum penderat in cruce, Pater ignosce illis. Sicut enim in Evangelio Nazarenorum habetur: ad hanc vocem Domini multa millia Judaeorum astantium circa crucem crediderunt." What does Haymo mean by telling us that " at this word of the Lord many thousands of Jews, who were standing around the Cross, believed?" The word of the Lord means the Prayer upon the Cross, and Haymo

[1] Migne P.L. 116. Col. 994.

tells us that this was in the Gospel according to the Nazarenes, with an additional statement of a highly rhetorical character that many thousand Jews believed on our Lord, in consequence of His prayer. By the Gospel according to the Nazarenes, there seems to be no doubt that Haymo means the lost early Gospel which commonly goes by the name of the Gospel according to the Hebrews. If that be the case then we have found a source to which we can refer the expansion made in the text of Luke, and so justify Dr. Hort's statement that it comes from an extraneous source. Or we can, if we please, say that the scribe who put it in Luke used the same source as did the Gospel of the Hebrews to which Haymo refers. But why should we multiply origins, when the Gospel to the Hebrews is early enough and sufficient to be responsible for the assumed quotation? Such an explanation would clear up all the textual difficulties and leave us in a good spirit of expectation that the whole of the missing Gospel may some day be recovered. I am surprised myself that it has eluded us so long.

In making this suggestion one will have to go further afield, and be prepared to

Speculations of Textual Criticism Justified. 101

raise more difficulties than one solves. It will be necessary to ask how Haymo knew this. Had he a copy of the Nazarene Gospel of which he speaks? It is hardly to be believed. It is more probable that in making his commentary on the prophet Isaiah, he did what all wise scribes of that time were accustomed to do, he brought out of his treasury things new and old, especially the latter. He must have had some lost commentary of antiquity at his disposal, at least in the form of extracts. And it ought to be possible to discover the commentator who preceded him. But then, as I say, we shall raise more difficulties than we solve: for the quotation in Haymo occurs in his commentary on Isaiah LIII., at the end of the chapter, and Haymo is showing that Christ fulfilled the prediction that " My righteous Servant *shall justify many* and He shall bear their iniquities." Now it is hardly possible to disconnect from this interpretation the closing words of the chapter in which the Servant of God is said " to have borne the sins of many, and to have *made intercession for the transgressors.*" In each case Haymo points out the conversion of the Jews. Thus the closing verses of Isaiah become a prediction of the Lord's prayer for His enemies, and of the immediate and striking result that was accomplished by that prayer. And it is at this point that the difficulty arises. We could very well admit that the Gospel to the Hebrews had fashioned an artificial fulfilment to the language of Isaiah LIII. in the conversion of many thousands of Jews who stood around the Cross: but it is quite another thing to admit the Prayer on the Cross to be itself an artificial fulfilment of the closing words of the great chapter. For the internal evidence is decisive against the belief that the whole of the passage in the Nazarene Gospel is from one hand. If it is a fabrication, there must be two fabricants. The man that invented the latter part cannot be the artist of the first part. Moreover it would be easy to show that pious persons in the second century were fulfilling prophecies for themselves. We have had an instance before us in this very lecture, in the new passage which has been found inserted among the last verses of Mark. Here our Lord is made to say (and the passage must be a fabrication), that "on account of those who sinned I was delivered over to death:" but this is an almost verbatim reproduction of the closing words of Isaiah LIII. in the

Greek of the LXX: (διὰ τὰς ἀνομίας αὐτῶν παρεδόθη *for their sins He was delivered up*; see also the preceding verses). Indeed it can hardly be denied that there was a tendency in certain quarters to manufacture details of fulfilled prophecy. So that in quoting Haymo, we are raising one of the most difficult exegetical problems. But whether we can at present resolve all these difficulties is not the immediate question. What is important is that, for the first time, an attempt has been made to identify the extraneous source whose existence Dr. Hort conjectured, in order to explain the curious relations of the MSS. to one another, and the absence of the incident we have been discussing from so many lines of textual transmission. So we make the hypothesis that the text of Luke has been glossed from the Gospel to the Hebrews by some well intentioned early scribe.

And now we are in a position to pass on to my third passage, the famous story of the adulteress, contained in John vii. 53—viii. 2.

3. You are familiar with the doubts that have been raised with regard to the authenticity of this passage. To begin with, it has no very early attestation in John, except in Western MSS., and

is absent from nearly all the great uncial MSS., and most of the early versions. Moreover it breaks the continuity of our Lord's discourse with the Jews and produces " a serious disruption in the incidents and discourses."[1] Accordingly Dr. Hort sums up the argument against the verses as follows:

" When the whole evidence is taken together, it becomes clear that the section first came into St. John's Gospel as an insertion in a comparatively late Western text, having originally belonged to an extraneous independent source. That this source was either the Gospel according to the Hebrews or the *Expositions of the Lord's Oracles* of Papias is a conjecture only: but it is a conjecture of high probability."

The reason for this conjecture lies in the fact, that Eusebius,[2] when giving an account of Papias, who flourished in the second century says that Papias " has likewise set forth another narrative concerning a woman who was calumniated before the Lord concerning many sins, which is contained in the Gospel according to the Hebrews."

The natural inference is that the section in John is borrowed either from Papias or from the

[1] Hort *Introd.* Notes p. 87.   [2] H.E. iii. 39. 16.

Gospel according to the Hebrews. Now here is a fresh consideration to which we wish to draw attention. There is a very famous group of cursive MSS. known to scholars as the Ferrar group, marked by many rare and many extraordinary readings: and in this group the section in question is inserted after Luke xxi. 38; no reason, that I know of, has ever been assigned for the transfer, unless it be that it finds a somewhat similar setting in Luke to what it normally does in John, in the statement that "the people came to Jesus very early in the morning to the temple to be taught."

My friend, Dr. Blass, was persuaded that the real home of the passage was in Luke, and printed it so in his edition of that Gospel. And when one reflects that we have already had reasons to believe that Luke was, at a very early date, glossed from the Gospel according to the Hebrews, that some MSS. of Luke are certainly glossed with a story, which on other accounts has been referred to the same Gospel, it does not seem an unreasonable thing to suggest that the same hand which inserted the Prayer on the Cross may have inserted the story of the adulteress in the same Gospel, which perhaps had a short life in that connexion, but afterwards in the West was taken up into John's Gospel where it found a home, until the textual critics of later days were strong enough to dislodge it.

It would be the height of folly to dogmatize over matters of this kind. But in any case we have fairly good evidence as to the source from which this story came: and perhaps these three illustrations may suffice to show how time deals with the difficulties raised by textual criticism, and vindicates against rash utterances and violent objurgations, the soundness of the methods and the trustworthiness of the results arrived at by the masters in this particular art and craft. Perhaps if we should succeed before long in finding either the lost works of Papias or the lost Gospel according to the Hebrews, many things that have been perplexing us as to passages in the New Testament that seem too loosely attached to their contexts and too feebly attested by ancient authorities, would become perfectly lucid to us. For in these larger matters which involve the removal of whole sections or verses, the same rule holds as applies to lesser variations, that "when the cause of a variant is known, the variant itself disappears."

APPENDIX TO LECTURE III.

Something was said in the foregoing Lecture about the extent to which fulfilments of prophecy have been manufactured by the writers of uncanonical gospels, such for example as the Peter Gospel, the Gospel according to the Hebrews, the Apocryphal Gospels relating to the birth and boyhood of Jesus, &c., and the question is still an unsettled one whether, and if so, how far, we ought to recognize a similar influence to be at any point at work in the Canonical Gospels. To deal with such a question thoroughly would require a whole course of lectures and would certainly bring up some critical situations of great interest. But as this is not the place for an extended inquiry into a collateral issue, however interesting, I will confine myself to a single instance which has recently come to light, in which many of the links in a chain of what I call prophetical gnosis can be clearly made out.

Suppose, for example, we were reading the account of the Mockery of Jesus at His trial before Pilate, and we should find in Mark xiv. 65 the following statement:

"And some of them began to spit upon Him and to cover His face and to buffet Him, and to say to Him: Prophesy, and the underlings received Him with blows: and they were striking Him on the head with a reed and spitting upon Him."

Now let us see how these incidents of the Passion are recorded in the Peter Gospel; of which we have a large fragment preserved from a grave in Egypt. Here we find as follows.

"And others standing by were spitting on His face, and others gave Him blows on His cheeks, others were pricking Him with a reed, and some were scourging Him and saying This is the honour with which we will honour the Son of God."

Now it is not difficult to detect a certain process of expansion of the narrative as we pass from Mark to Peter, as for instance when the words, "and some of them began to spit on Him" are explained in the sense that "others

Appendix to Lecture III.

of the bystanders began to spit on His face," the expansion being obvious and natural. But it is not so clear why the general statement that they were buffeting Him (according to Mark) and that they were striking Him on the head with a reed (Mark) should appear in Peter in the form that they gave Him blows on the cheeks and pricked Him with a reed. And we might hazard a conjecture that these transitions show the influence of a passage in Micah (iv. 14) which tells us "that they shall smite the judge of Israel with a rod upon the cheeks": the cheeks being read into the Marcan narrative in order to make the parallel.

At first sight this seems a little artificial, and the question might be asked why a reference to Micah and the prophetic gnosis is necessary at all. Let us see if there is any evidence of the employment of the passage from Micah in the sense which I have intimated.

Amongst certain Manichaean documents which have recently come to light from Chinese Turkestan, of which I shall be speaking presently, there are some old Persian fragments containing the account of the Passion: from these we find the following sentences decipherable, the matter being apparently a harmony of certain Gospels:

> "A crown of thorns set on His head
> . . . .
> With a reed they smite Him on the cheeks,
> On His eyes (? face) they spit,
> And they call out 'Our Lord Messiah.'"

Here we are very near indeed to the actual passage from the Prophet. Perhaps the writer has used the Peter Gospel, but if so, he has brought the language closer to that of Micah. So we have again the suggestion of prophetic gnosis. The argument is not final, the proof is incomplete. But it is at all events suggestive that we should find from the far East an unexpected confirmation to a theory which has been evolved in order to explain the relations between Mark's Gospel (considered as primitive) and the Peter Gospel (generally regarded as a product of the second century and strongly coloured by prophetical gnosis).

LECTURE IV.

THE ROMANCE OF THE VERSIONS.

ONE of the first things that a student learns when he begins the critical study of the New Testament, is that the materials for the determination of the text consist of Copies, Versions and Fathers—that the original text is known to us by Transcripts, by Translations and by Transferences. And when the historical development of the science of N.T. criticism is under review, it will soon be seen that it is only by slow degrees and with much hesitation that the factors supplied by the Versions and the Fathers have been allowed weight in the determination of the right readings. We began indeed, in these islands, with a version which practically passed for the original, both among the Saxons and the early English, as indeed the Latin Vulgate still does where religion is regulated by infallible authority. But those were the days when Textual Criticism was in its very infancy. Wyclif does not encumber his margins with disputes over the spelling of Bethesda or with references to what " some ancient authorities say." Even Tyndale who is close to the great revival of Biblical studies does not use his margins for that form of edification: he has something much more amusing to say, about the Pope's Bull devouring more than Aaron's Calf, with enquiries as to when the Pope is going to cry Hoo! i.e., Hold, and stop building St. Peter's. But while Wyclif's object is to render the Latin Vulgate into English, Tyndale's object is to get away from the Latin version to the original Greek; and it is only gradually, under a mixed influence of reaction and of learning, that scholars have come back to realise the importance of the Vulgate in the determination of the text, and still more the importance of those earlier Latin versions which preceded the Vulgate and are often our surest guides to the forms in which the Greek New Testament once circulated. How slowly, too, did the Syriac Version find its way into the West, and into due appreciation of scholars. Its first edition is the Vienna volume of 1555; but that is five years later than the great folio New Testament of Stephen which held its own for so long a time, as the standard text to which all reference should be made, of which Bentley ironically said that Pope Stephen's text stood as if an apostle had been his compositor. But Bentley, himself, who planned to reform the New Testament Text by means of a combination of Greek MSS. and Latin Versions, had no suspicion of the extent to which scholars in later days would defer to the evidence that should be brought from the Euphrates or the Nile.

The Coptic Version had a better welcome; it found its way into the textual apparatus before even it got into print, and was employed by Bishop Fell in his notes, more than thirty years before it appeared as an edition. It found a place, too, in the notes to Mill's great edition, again before the actual publication of the version. So there were some up-to-date Biblical scholars in England, before Agamemnon! Around these great versions, the Syriac, Egyptian and Latin, and the later versions that are affiliated with them, there gathers not a little of romance and a good deal of mystery. We can see great figures looming through the mist of the past, or suspect them, where the veil is too thick to be actually penetrated. We are sure that the work was inspired by Kings, Sages, and Saints; for we can often come across their traces; the orthodox churchman is to the front, but so is the heretic and the Arian; and sometimes people of servile origin and lowly station stand out, as having with great toil and difficulty enriched whole populations with the words of life. One has only to think of Ulfilas, the Apostle of the Goths, of Frumentius and Aedesius, the captives of the Abyssinians; of Tatian, the Assyrian (to whom we owe the text of the Diatessaron); of Rabbula, the Bishop of Edessa (to whom belongs, in all probability, the honour of the Peshito text, one of the most beautiful, perhaps the most beautiful, of all the translations of the New Testament). Or to come down to more modern times, we may think of Alfred the Great and the venerable Bede, and see how wide an array of great personalities is open to us, and how varied have been the experiences and fortunes of the translators. But it must not be forgotten that there is still much that is elusive and mysterious about the subject of the Versions; the authors of the early Latin translations are altogether unknown to us, until we come to Jerome: the first translator of the separate Gospels into Syriac is still a mystery, and will probably remain so; and as far as I know there is not a vestige of evidence as to the translators of the early Egyptian versions. So that, from the historical point of view, we run into a cloud, as we try to penetrate to the origin of either of the three great lines of versions of the New Testament, and the same thing will be true of not a few of the lesser and later translations that have come to light.

In the present Lecture I propose to raise two questions with regard to the diffusion of the Gospel in Asia, and to draw your attention to one new Asiatic version which has recently come to light. I am going to ask whether there is any reason to suspect that the Gospel was, at an early date, translated into (a) the Chinese language; (b) into any one of the Indian languages; and I am going to tell you of the discovery of a translation of the New Testament into the language of a people on the further side of Siberia, and on the very borders of China. We will take the last point first, as it has a bearing upon the other two questions, apart from its own particular interest.

In the year 1903 there were found in Chinese Turkestan, by a German explorer named Grünwedel, a variety of MSS. written in a Syriac hand. He acquired them, either by purchase or by actual exploration, from a place named Turfan. Some of them were written on paper, others on white leather or on silk, but though written in a Syriac alphabet, they were not in the Syriac language, but in old Persian or in Turcoman, and they contained a variety of writings belonging to the heresy of Mani the Persian, which we know by the name of Manichaean. Upon the doctrines of Mani and his followers these MSS. are destined to throw great light: for amongst them are portions of Mani's own gospel, and epistles: then there are fragments of a Christian Gospel closely related to the Gospel of Peter, and of a Passion Gospel which appears to be related to the Harmony of Tatian. Further, there are hymns and prayers of the Manichees which illustrate their doctrines and ritual and will enable us to re-write the history of that wide-spread heresy, which once counted Augustine amongst its followers: and there is a portion of Mani's own work, which he called by the name of Shapurakan. The importance of all this is evident. For Mani is one of the most mysterious figures of the early church; it is marvellous that one man, a heretic from the Christian standpoint, and still more a heretic and proscribed person from the standpoint of the Zoroastrian religion, should have succeeded in spreading a new dualistic faith, which borrowed from both Christianity and Parsism, over every country which he visited, including perhaps both China and India. These Turkestan documents are from the tenth century, but they may perhaps imply that Manichaeism had been there from the third century under the apostolate of Mani himself. This physician from Babylon is a very wizard in religious propagandism, and stands on a level with Mahomet himself. We, have, then, a wealth of new evidence for the study of Manichaeism, and we find, as I have said, the great heresy occupying Chinese Turkestan as far back as the tenth century and no one can say for how many centuries before that. But what of Christianity itself? Behind the writings of Mani and his followers we see the Gospels, and the Syriac Gospels, too, in evidence: but up to the time of the first publication of these documents by Professor Müller, there was no trace, except these indirect evidences, of Syriac Gospels or Syriac Churches in these distant regions and at the early date which the Turfan discoveries suggest.

In August, 1905, however, there arrived in Berlin, addressed to Professor Sachau, eight photographs of leaves of four separate MSS. They were accompanied by a letter, sent apparently from a station on the Siberian Railway by an archeologist who was engaged in the explorations in Chinese Turkestan of which we have been speaking. The MSS. were written, three of them in the Syriac language, the fourth in Syriac characters with slight variations, but in an unknown tongue. The date of the MSS. was, to judge by the handwriting, of the ninth or tenth century, but as Professor Sachau was cautious enough to say that the writing of such outlying districts is apt (like the fashion of ladies' dresses in the country) to be a little archaic, perhaps we might have to depress the date a little from the first estimate. Of the unknown language he was able to conjecture that it belonged to the Iranian family and to identify a word or two here and there. For instance, when

The Romance of the Versions. 119

the letters *Pncmik* were expanded as *Pancamik*, even those who only know enough of the meaning of Indian words to tell that *Punjab* means *five rivers*, would have little difficulty in recognising the word for *fifth*; so here was a new language, related to our own, apparently at the furthest point in N.E. Asia that Indo-European speech has yet been discovered. The Syriac leaves, properly so called, contained portions of the Nestorian Church hymns for the ecclesiastical year, exactly as they were in use and as they are found in MSS. in the original settlements of the Nestorians in the Tigris Valley and on the frontiers of Persia. But what were Nestorians doing in this far away district amongst people of another language, and presumably of another race than themselves? It was probable that they were in close relations with them, for they were using their own alphabet with some modifications, to transcribe the words of the language of their neighbours. And this at once suggests the relation of teacher and taught, and that the outlying Indo-Iranian people had no written speech of their own. In that case the Nestorians must have been something more than transient guests. Is it possible that they were on a mission? They clearly had carried their religion with them, as far as their own souls were concerned: for here were the Church rituals and hymn-books. So there were interesting questions in the air, and it was natural to await with expectation the further reports of what Herr Albert von le Coq had found amongst the ruins of Turfan. Amongst those which have since been published in facsimile, or whose contents have been communicated to the Berlin Academy of Sciences, there was a long piece in the new language, to which I am now going to draw attention. As the district from which the text came is called by the ancient geographers Sogdiana, the language has been christened Sogdianese. The new piece of Sogdianese, then, was marked with vowels in the Nestorian manner, had also some traces of accentuation, and was evidently meant for reading aloud. At its close was a rubric in Syriac to the passage which was to follow:

"For the fourth Sunday of the month Kanun the former. From Matt. c. i.,"

from which it appears that we are dealing with a lectionary arranged according to the Syrian calendar. On looking over the passage which precedes, of which the heading is lost, it was easy to find something that could be made out: for instance here were the words

'at sôqant qat χvardàrat qu-'Abraham mâχ pitri-sâ.

Here it is clear that we have something to do with Abraham our father, and bearing in mind that the next lesson has to do with the opening of Matthew and the beginning of the life of Christ, it is not hard to make the successful guess that here we have a bit of the hymn of Zacharias, "*And the oath which he sware to our father Abraham.*"

The passage was a translation of Luke i. 63-80. So now we could go to work and study the new language and make out its grammar and dictionary. Here the decipherers were greatly helped by another leaf which contained a passage from Galatians iii. in a double transcription, Syriac in one column, and Sogdianese in an adjoining column. So the working out of the grammar, etc., went on merrily, and we do not feel so far away from home when we learn that

$$\begin{aligned} \text{I am} &= \text{'im} \\ \text{thou art} &= \text{'iš} \\ \text{he is} &= \text{χaci} \end{aligned}$$

or that we are, you are, and they are, are represented by 'istâ, 'ista, χant which you can compare with the Greek, and Latin forms. Many words can be at once identified by their Sanskrit and Persian parallels: and sometimes a plain Englishman can see what is meant. So it is clear that the Nestorians had translated the New Testament into Sogdianese, and had taught the natives the alphabet and the doctrine. One more achievement to be reckoned to that great missionary Church!

The Nestorians had been expelled from the Roman Empire on account of their refusal to call the Blessed Virgin the Mother of God (a noble and far reaching protest), and on account of their recognising two distinct natures in Christ, and now they had turned to the Gentiles and were filling a continent with their doctrine.

Whatever date we assign to these MSS. from the ninth century to the eleventh, they imply a previous occupation of Sogdiana by Nestorian missionaries. And we cannot well dissociate the conversion of this district from the still greater task which lay geographically before them, the conquest of China for Christ, and other work which must have been done by them on their travels eastward from Mesopotamia and the Persian Gulf. It was a campaign of deliberate conquest, one of the greatest that Christian missionaries have ever planned. We might be quite certain that they did not pass through Persia without translating the Scriptures into the language of the people to whose tolerance they owed their very life, nor neglect the populations through whom they passed. As a matter of fact, we have evidence on these points. For if we want to get an idea of the extent of the Nestorian propaganda in Central Asia and China, we have only to take the documentary evidence of the division of these lands into provinces and dioceses. In the year 1265 the Nestorians reckoned twenty-five Asiatic provinces and more than seventy dioceses. Amongst the latter were Transoxiana, Turkestan, China and Tangout. Tangout comprised the part of Western China now known as Shensi and Kansu, and the capital of the province was Hsi'en-fu where a great inscription was discovered to which we shall presently refer. From Marco Polo and other travellers we get information of the existence of Nestorian Churches all along the trade routes from Bagdad to Pekin.[1]

From the foregoing it appears probable that

[1] See Bonin in *Journal Asiatique*, ix serie, tom 15, p. 584.

from quite early times there was a steady output of translations into Old Persian on the part of the Nestorian Church, and we need have not the least hesitation in saying that these translations must have included the Scriptures; and if they translated the New Testament at the early date indicated, the version is probably not yet published, as the existing Persian texts do not seem to be of any great antiquity. In view of the extent of literary work covered by the Nestorian translators, coupled with the fact that we find the Nestorian Commentators quoting the Diatessaron as late as the ninth century, it is interesting to reflect that there is a possibility that we may come upon the lost Diatessaron in one of these outlying translations, a point on which we shall have something to say presently.

Now supposing we have located rightly the activity of the Nestorian scholars and teachers in Sogdiana, let us look at the map and see how far afield it is to Hsi'en-fu, within the Chinese Empire where we next come across the Nestorians, and find a very famous monument erected to commemorate the conversion of China to nominal Christianity in the seventh century of our era. Instead of beginning with the study of the actual monument, of which I am so fortunate as to possess a splendid rubbing, obtained by the deputation of the Baptist Mission (Mr. Wilson and Mr. Fullerton) who recently visited the place—I propose to begin with a very late and curious tradition which I came across in a modern Greek Synaxarion, or Summary of the Lives of the Saints, arranged for the course of the Ecclesiastical Year. Here under the date October 6th, I found a sketch of the labours of the Apostle Thomas, running something as follows:

ἐπροχώρησε καὶ ἕως εἰς τὴν Κίναν, ἢ Σίναν τὴν ἀνατωλικωτάτην. ὅθεν καὶ ἀναγινώσκομεν εἰς τὴν Γεωγραφίαν τοῦ Φατζέα, ὅτι ἐν τῷ πολυθρυλλήτῳ πύργῳ καὶ πολυτιμήτῳ ὁμοῦ (καθότι εἶναι ὅλος ἀπὸ ἄνωθεν ἕως κάτω ᾠκοδομημένος ἐκ σινικοῦ κεράμου, ἐν τούτῳ, λέγω, τῷ πύργῳ γεγραμμημένα εἰσὶ τὰ λόγια ταῦτα. Διὰ τοῦ θείου Θωμᾶ ἡ οὐράνιος πίστις ἐξαπέπτη, καὶ εἰς Σινῶν (πόλιν δηλ. ἢ ἐπαρχίαν) παρεγένετο.

He (Thomas) went on as far as the furthest east of Kina or China; wherefore also we read in the geography of Fatzéa, that in the renowned tower (a costly one, too, for it is all built from top to bottom of Chinese porcelain: in this tower, I say,) are recorded the following words: By the divine Thomas the Heavenly Faith was sent forth and it reached China's (city or province).

Here then we have a tradition which the Synaxarist borrows from some modern Greek geography (of which I am unable to find a copy) that there was a famous monument of porcelain containing an inscription that St. Thomas sent the Faith into China. And the Synaxarist explains this to mean that St. Thomas himself visited China in his missionary travels. Now with regard to this tradition, it seems clear that the reference is ultimately to the famous monument of Hsi'en-fu, and the reference to St. Thomas is very instructive; obviously it arises out of the fact that St. Thomas is the patron-saint of the Church of Syria, or at least of Edessa, which is the starting point for the first eastward migrations. That St. Thomas preached in China is merely one more case to be added to many others of the migration of traditions. Its single foundation lies in the fact that Nestorian missionaries converted China to Christianity. We shall see the importance of this when we come to a somewhat similar case, the preaching of St. Thomas in India.

And now let us look at the monument itself,

and the very important chronological date which it presents. The inscription is in Chinese, but is flanked and bordered by Syriac writing in a beautiful hand of the eight century: to judge from the fact that Chinese literati make pilgrimages to the province of Shensi in order to copy the characters of the inscription, the Chinese writing must be as exquisitely classical as the Syriac is. Hsi'en-fu is the name of the district in which the monument is found, and the actual city is called Chang'an. There are many other famous monuments in this city, amongst them a set of stone tablets of the Confucian Classics, engraved in the years 833—837 A.D. You will find in Dr. Legge's lecture on the Inscription, published under the title of *Christianity in China*, an account of the discovery of the monument in 1625 and of the way in which its text came into the hands of the Jesuit missionaries. It is an astonishing thing and betrays a very discreditable spirit of scepticism that this discovery should have been challenged in the West as a fabrication of the Jesuits and that amongst the names of those who disputed its genuineness Bishop Horne is found side by side with Voltaire and Renan. On the other hand Gibbon saw clearly what was the meaning of the inscription and tells us that "the Christianity of China between the seventh and the thirteenth century is invincibly proved by the consent of Chinese, Arabian, Syriac and Latin evidence. The inscription of Si-gan-fu which describes the fortunes of the Nestorian Mission from the first mission A.D. 636 to the current year 781, is accused of forgery by La Croze,[1] Voltaire, etc., who become the dupes of their own cunning, whilst they are afraid of a Jesuitical fraud." The dates which are given are obtained both from the Chinese text and from the Syriac borderings: the latter say it is the year 1092 according to the reckoning of the Greeks, i.e. the year 781 of our era:[2] the

[1] La Croze did not deny the existence of a Christian Church in China: cf. La Croze, *Histoire du Christianisme des Indes*. i. 62: "Pour ce qui est de'l ancien Christianisme connu et preché dans le Royaume de la Chine, il me semble qu'il y auroit de la tèmèrité a le nier. Marc Paul en fait mention, et les premiers Missionaires de Jésuites en ont trouvé quelques vestiges. D'ailleurs les livres Ecclesiastiques des Malabares et leurs anciennes Ecritures faisant mention de l'Eveque qu'on y envoyoit autrefois de Babylone, il semble qu'il n'y a point de lieu d'en douter. A ces preuves je n'oserois ajouter l'Inscription deterrée l'an 1625 dans la Ville de Siganfu, capitale de la Province de Xensi. C'est une piéce manifestement supposée comme je l'ai fait voir ailleurs."

[2] In the year 1092 of the Greeks my Lord Yezdbuzid,

Chinese text gives us the date of the arrival of the Mission. The first missionary is named Olopun, a name which I cannot identify, he is called the greatly virtuous Olopun and he is said to come from the West, from the Kingdom of Ta Ts'in.

" Guiding himself by the azure clouds, he carried with him the true Scriptures. Watching the laws of the winds, he made his way through difficulties and through perils. In the ninth year of the period Chang-Kwan (A.D. 635) he arrived at Chang'an. The emperor sent his minister, Duke Fang Hsüan-ling, bearing the staff of office, to the western suburb, there to receive the visitor, and conduct him to the palace. The Scriptures were translated in the Library. (His Majesty) questioned him about his system in his own forbidden apartments, became deeply convinced of its correctness and truth, and gave special orders for its propagation."

It may, I think, be inferred that the greatly virtuous Olopun was already acquainted with the Chinese language, for there is no reason to

Presbyter and Chorepiscopos of Kumdan (i.e. Chang'an) the royal city, son of the departed Meles, Presbyter of Balkh, City of Tahuristan, erected this stone tablet, etc.

suppose that the Emperor and his staff knew Syriac. And if Olopun was capable of translating his sacred books at sight into Chinese, and of holding a prolonged religious conference with the Emperor, it would be absurd to suppose that he neglected his opportunity to make a Chinese translation of the sacred books which he had brought with him. What happened on a small scale in Sogdiana must have been repeated on a large scale in China, and I fail to see the reason why some of these early Chinese Scriptures should not be found when we have found Scriptures in the wilderness outside the Flowery Land. Whether the Chinese Mission preceded or followed the mission to Sogdiana, we may not be able to determine with certainty. But as it is all on one line of march and good generals do not leave unreduced fortresses in their rear, we may, if we please, put the Mission to Sogdiana first. The steady pressure which was driving the Nestorians eastward may be seen by the illustration of the Syrian ecclesiastic who erected the tablet; his father was a priest in the City of Balkh. The motto in those days must have been, " Go East, young Christian, go East," and it is a valid motto yet. That

Olopun brought his books with him appears from the further description of the great interview, which resulted, three years later, in an imperial proclamation to the following effect:

"Systems have not always the same name. Sages have not always the same personality. Every religion has its appropriate doctrines which by their imperceptible influence benefit the inhabitants. The greatly virtuous Olopun of the Kingdom of Ta Tsin, *bringing his Scriptures and his images from afar*, has come and presented them at our high Capital. Having carefully examined the scope of his doctrine, we find them to be mysterious, admirable and requiring nothing (special) to be done; having looked at the principal and most honoured points in them, they are intended for the establishment of what is most important. Their language is free from troublesome verbosity; their principles remain when the immediate occasion for their delivery is forgotten; (the system) is helpful to (all) creatures and profitable for men—let it have free course throughout the Empire."

Amongst those books it is reasonable to suppose that the complete New Testament was included; for the author of the inscription in summing up the doctrine of Christianity says of our Lord that "when His mighty work was thus completed, at noon-day He ascended to His true place. He left behind Him the twenty-seven standard books. These set forth the great conversion for the deliverance of the soul." The number twenty-seven exactly covers our present New Testament: but as the Peshito does not contain four of the Catholic Epistles, or the Revelation, I should hesitate to believe that this is all that is meant by the inscription; it is possible that there may be some added volumes —perhaps of Canons, or of Clementine or other Apocrypha. The number, however, is so strikingly coincident that we may be sure the Syrians brought their New Testament with them. That they brought other books as well may perhaps be inferred from the description of the country of Tâ Ts'in from which the Christian Embassy was supposed to have come, a land "where robberies and thefts are unknown among the common people: where men enjoy happiness and peace: where none but the Illustrious Religion is observed, none but virtuous rulers are appointed: a territory of vast extent *whose literary productions are brilliant.*"

I find it hard to believe that all the literature imported by the Nestorians and all the books translated by them can have perished. Somewhere, perhaps, in the corners of the Buddhist temples that succeeded to the Christian monasteries, there may be lurking Syriac and Chinese MSS., or Syro-Chinese bilingual MSS., which would add greatly to our knowledge of the Nestorian Church and of the Christian literature. If such exist, they cannot, from the nature of the case, be of late date; and they may be very early. For Dr. Legge thought that the Nestorian movement had received its death-blow by an Imperial edict of A.D. 845. So that any surviving MSS. could not be later than the ninth century and may be as old as we like reasonably to imagine. I notice that Dr. Legge does not think that much translation on the part of the first missionaries can be inferred, and that probably only select passages were invoked, but I submit that, after the evidence from Sogdiana, this suggestion has lost its verisimilitude; I see no reason why the Diatessaron itself should not turn up in China.

And having reached that point, I will confess that my optimism once reached the point of believing I had found it. It came about in this way. Many who are acquainted with the early stages of the Christian campaign for the conquest of China, will remember that Morrison began his studies, preliminary to the translation of the New Testament into Chinese, by working at a Chinese Harmony of the Gospels which was in the British Museum: this Harmony he ultimately made the base of his first Chinese New Testament. Besides this, the translation contained the Acts of the Apostles and the Pauline Epistles, with the exception of Hebrews. Looked at from the outside, that has the appearance of being an early canon of Scripture. The impression this translation made upon Morrison may be seen from his memoirs (compiled by his widow, London, 1839):

p. 67. "The British and Foreign Bible Society, almost from its formation, had the claims of China before it: and having been informed that a MS. version of the New Testament in the Chinese language was deposited in the British Museum, entertained thoughts of printing it: but, on further enquiry the idea was relinquished." [1]

[1] The reason for this was that they knew it to be a Harmony,

p. 77. "After he had acquired the method of writing Chinese, and some degree of familiarity with the characters, he commenced the transcription of the Chinese MS. in the British Museum, which has already been mentioned, containing a Harmony of the Gospels, the Acts of the Apostles, and all the Pauline Epistles except that of the Hebrews."

p. 78. "Speaking of his endeavours to prepare himself for his work, Dr. Milne says, 'what was acquired of the language proved afterwards of very trifling utility. The Dictionary and the Harmony of the Gospels, were more useful. They were originally the work of some Roman missionaries in China. By what individuals or at what time, these works were compiled, has not been ascertained; but Providence had preserved them to be useful, and the just merits of their authors will doubtless one day be reckoned to them.'"

It is not quite easy to say how Dr. Milne was so sure the Harmony came from Roman hands, when he had no clue either to the hands

and not a text of the Gospels. Mr. Canton, in his *History of the Bible Society,* says that they had also ascertained from experts that it was based upon the Vulgate. See Canton, *l.c.* i. 24 and 299.

themselves or to the period of their activity.

Morrison took his copy of the Harmony to China with them and used to set his assistants and domestics to read therefrom on the Lord's Day and he tells us that "My assistant is of opinion that the translation which I have of the Gospel and Epistles (which I brought from England) was made by some Chinese: the style being better than he supposed could be produced by any foreigner." In his letters to the Directors of the London Missionary Society, he frequently alludes to the famous MS. of which he had a further transcript made by one of his assistants, as follows:

"I have also Low Hëen, whom I mentioned before; he transcribed for me the Harmony of the Gospels and the Acts of the Apostles. He put them into the form of Chinese books, which they had not before, &c."

"In September I sent the Acts of the Apostles, carefully revised with the Greek text, corrected and pointed, to a Chinese printer, and after having a specimen of his workmanship, engaged for 1,000 copies. I am to have the blocks, which if cut on good wood, according to our agreement, will strike off 15,000 copies before they need be repaired and after that the plates may be used for a greater or less period of time. How many they will strike off before they are absolutely useless I cannot say. The terms are 521 dollars," &c.

And again in a letter from Canton on January 11th, 1814:

"I beg to inform the Society that the translation of the New Testament, carrying on at this place, into the Chinese language, has been completed, and I hourly expect the last sheet from the press. . . . . The Gospel, the closing Epistles and the Book of Revelation, are entirely my own translating. The middle part of the volume is founded on the work of some unknown individual, whose pious labours were deposited in the British Museum. I took the liberty of altering and supplying what appeared to me to be requisite; and I feel great pleasure in recording the benefit which I first derived from the labours of my unknown predecessor."

These are some of the passages in which Morrison speaks of the MS. which contained the Harmony. I cannot see that he ever himself refers the work to Roman or Jesuit hands.[1]

[1] The actual MS. in the British Museum has the following

This, then, is what I went in quest of, with a desire to obtain some information as to the nature of the text and the character of the Harmony that was translated. But, as so often happens in these matters, the scent became cold, and after conference with Professor Giles, of Cambridge, and the examination of some passages together, I came to the conclusion that some Western Harmony, perhaps one of the many Latin Harmonies, lies at the back of the MS. It would be interesting to have some further light thrown on this point: the translation itself, when done back into English, is very fresh and racy.

And now let us retrace our steps, bearing in mind the information that we have acquired, our convictions as to the splendid zeal and enthusiasm of the Nestorian Church, and of their skill in transferring their spiritual oracles into the tongues of surrounding peoples and nations. We are now to ask the question, What about India? Was there ever an early planting of

note: "Evangelia Quatuor Sinice MS. This transcript was made at Canton in 1738 and 1739, by order of Mr. Hodgson, Jr. [of the East India Company], who says it has been collated with care and found very correct. Given by him to Sir Hans Sloan in September, 1739." But this tells nothing about the ancestry of the MS., nor the original composer.

Christianity in India? And if so was it effective? Was it the work of the Nestorians? Or was it earlier? And if it was earlier, was it in any way re-inforced by Nestorian activity? The problem is a very interesting one, for it may be approached in so many different ways. We might begin with the facts, or with the traditions, or with the *à priori* probabilities of the case. The facts are the existence to this day of a Syrian Church in Malabar, claiming direct descent from St. Thomas, and possessing a certain amount of Syriac literature in their archives, but using the Malayalam language in their every-day intercourse. A similar Church once existed in Madras, where it has been displaced (what was left of it) by the Roman Catholics. The traditions are two-fold, one the written legends of the preaching and death of St. Thomas, especially the book known as the Syriac Acts of Judas Thomas the Apostle, according to which Thomas, or rather Judas Thomas, is sold by our Lord to a certain Indian merchant, and goes to India to build a palace for the king of the country. The other tradition of Christian preaching in India is a precise one and comes to us through Eusebius, who tells us that Pantaenus the Christian philosopher and teacher of Clement of Alexandria, the founder of the famous school at Alexandria, had actually made the journey to India, and found traces of the preaching of the Apostle Bartholomew, and that Bartholomew had left in the country the Hebrew Gospel of Matthew (about which Gospel the Fathers talk so much and so obscurely).[1] These are the two forms of tradition which we are called upon to harmonize.

As to the probabilities of the case we may say that they are very high for a belief in Nestorian missions to India: for the people that found China by a long overland journey of many months over countries most inconvenient of transit, could hardly have neglected what was practically their next-door neighbour by sea. The trade-route, whether by land or sea, has always been the line of advance of the Gospel.

Now let us turn from the *à priori* probabilities to the facts. We do find such a Church still existing in Malabar. It has been the subject, in our time, of a very famous conflict in which

---

[1] This tradition is transcribed by Jerome and amplified in his characteristic manner. What he adds to the Eusebian tradition is probably agreeable fiction.

The Romance of the Versions. 141

the two rival branches of the Syrian Church, the Jacobite or Western, and the Nestorian or Eastern, fought out their rights of control over the native churches in India before an Anglo-Indian Court. What happened in the decision of the case was something like what happened recently when Scotch Churchmen came to England for the settlement of their internal strife: the Court took the wrong view, and I believe, as a matter of fact, its judgment has since been reversed. It gave the Syrian churches in India to the Jacobites. But a little study of archeology would have shown that they were Nestorian churches. The oldest churches in the Malabar and Madras districts contain crosses surrounded by old Persian inscriptions: so the churches must have been under Nestorian administration and governed from Seleucia-Ktesiphon on the Tigris. We may regard the Syriac and Old Persian languages as the two languages of the Christians in these districts, the one being the language of ecclesiastical government, the other the language of the temporal control to which they deferred. There is no trace of any vernacular Indian Scripture, as far as I know, on these early monuments.

And this agrees closely with what we find in the travels of Kosmas Indicopleustes, who is our first trustworthy authority for Christianity in Southern India, that "even in the Island of Ceylon, in the Indian Sea, there is a Church of Christians with clergy and a congregation of believers, though I know not if there be any Christians further in that direction. And such also is the case in the land called Malabar, where the pepper grows. And in the place called Cabana, there is a bishop appointed from Persia:" and he tells us, in speaking again of Ceylon that "the island hath also a Church of Persian Christians who have settled there, and a presbyter who is appointed from Persia, and all the apparatus of public worship; but the natives and their rulers are heathens."

This evidence is of the highest importance; it fixes the date of the colonization of the various places in Southern India as something anterior to A.D. 522 when Cosmas made his Indian journey; it shows the Churches as colonies, rather than as successful missions, that is, in an early stage of development; and it furnishes these statements on the faith of a man who knew Persia and is believed to have been himself a Nestorian.

When we take the early sixth century evidence of Kosmas with the seventh century evidence of the Madras and Malabar Churches, we can have little doubt that the Christianity of Southern India in those days (and some of it which has continued to our own) is Nestorian Christianity of the same period as that of the great missionary movement which took the Nestorians across the Continent of Asia to China at the beginning of the seventh century.

It is curious, however, that amongst these Churches we do not now come across any early traces, as yet, of vernacular Scripture, nor of the translation of sacred books, such as we find in Sogdiana. It is, of course, possible that the Persian Syrians went to India for trading purposes as well as for religious ends, and perhaps this may have been the direction in which their energy was drawn off. Kosmas' one bishop in Ceylon is a different figure from the long tale of Syrian ecclesiastics who decorate the Hsiën-fu monument. Moreover there is conclusive evidence that for many years they were re-inforced by immigration from the Persian Gulf and not by proselytism only. we may confidently refer the history of Christianity in Southern India to a Nestorian origin.[1]

The questions that remain are concerned with the legends of the preaching of St. Thomas and St. Bartholomew.

I have no space to deal exhaustively with the two traditions which ascribe the origin of Indian Christianity to St. Thomas and St. Bartholomew. In favour of the former there is the identification of the King Gundophar, with a first century ruler of Cabul and the Punjab, of whom many coins are extant. There is no doubt as to the existence of a real Gundophar, and if he is the person in the Thomas legends, the India of those legends is, at the furthest, the Punjab, to the west of India; at the nearest, the outlying portions of the Parthian Empire. For the "coins of Gundophar are common in Cabul and Candahar, and in Seistan and in the Western and Southern Punjab."[2]

In my judgment, the identification of Gundophar is not enough to float the Thomas legends

[1] The best book on the Syrian Church in India is a work under that title by Mr. Milne Rae. It is sometimes spoken of disparagingly by such as are "insolent to maintain tradition," but that is not necessarily a demerit.

[2] Cunningham: *Journal of Asiatic Society* xxiii., pp. 711, 712, quoted by Milne Rae: p. 364.

to the level of history. He was evidently a ruler of great force and influence who had caught the popular imagination, and was likely to turn up in the apocryphal story which connected the Church of Edessa with Churches on the farther frontier of Parthia. But, if we concede the possible existence of such Churches, we know too much about St. Thomas from the internal analysis of the Apocryphal Acts to regard him as anything else than a substitute for the Heavenly Twins, who were, in those days, the patron deities of Edessa.

With regard to the supposed mission of Bartholomew which was said to have been attested by Pantaenus, I should like to speak with more reserve. It has about it some elements of verisimilitude. I am not one of those people who wish to minimize the historical intercourse between India and Alexandria: it is possible that people travelled to India, more than occasionally, before the Suez Canal was opened and before the establishment of the P. & O. line of steamships. But the story is suspicious, in the same way in which the Thomas mission is suspicious. It contains a suggestion of apostolical authority for some persons unknown, and this is the most dangerous way that history takes of saying "I am of Paul" and "I of Cephas." The India of which Pantaenus speaks may be, however, the real India, as he seems to have had some knowledge of the Brahmins: and if he did not take this from books, we may have to admit something like an Indian mission by Pantaenus in the latter part of the second century. But we are not able to clear the matter up, for want of sufficient evidence and corroboration.

However, we have now gone over the ground, and we conclude that there is no prospect of recovering an early Indian Bible, as we think there may be of recovering early Chinese Scriptures. We have drawn attention to the marvellous activity of the Nestorian Church: they have long since shrunk to the merest remnant in the mountains of Kurdistan: "the wild-boar out of the wood has wasted them;" their Paradise has returned to the wilderness. But we cannot think of their remnant without interior motions of compassion and regret. "Men are we, and must grieve when e'en the shade of that which once was great has passed away." Christians are we, and must grieve over unsuccessful attacks on the rulers of the darkness of this world. For as Gibbon so justly and so honestly argued, " the zeal of the Nestorians overleaped the limits which had confined the ambition and curiosity both of the Greeks and Persians. The missionaries of Balkh and Samarcand pursued without fear the footsteps of the roving Tartar." Their passion to preach Christ where he had not been named was worthy of St. Paul himself, and their decline and almost complete disappearance is one of the mysterious features of Ecclesiastical History.

LECTURE V.

SIDE-LIGHTS ON THE AUTHORSHIP OF THE EPISTLE TO THE HEBREWS.

IN the present Lecture I propose to leave the fields of Textual Criticism and of Archeology, where I have been trying to test ancient beliefs by new discoveries. We have tried to excavate in Jerusalem the right text of John v. 2; to unearth new endings of Mark in Egypt; to decipher fresh translations of the Syriac New Testament in Siberia; but now let us leave the region of external research, and try a simple problem of authorship, unencumbered by a great deal of critical apparatus or theories of genealogical relation of the great MSS. Perhaps in the problem which I propose to undertake I may not refer to any variation of the text at all, except in one direction, viz., I may suggest some slight alterations in the forms or arrangements of the words: that is, I shall resort occasionally to conjectural emendation. I am aware that until quite recent years this was considered a prohibited practice. For example, when Bentley brought out his proposals for the great folio edition of the New Testament, in which all the errors were to be cleared up, he expressly disowned conjectural emendation in the following terms:

"The author is very sensible, that in the sacred writings there's no place for conjectures or emendations. Diligence and fidelity, with some judgment and experience are the characters here requisite. He declares, therefore, that he does not alter one letter in the text without the authorities subjoined in the notes."

When one reflects upon Bentley's astonishing skill in the restoration of a corrupt classical text in Greek or Latin, it is certain that it required a great deal of self-denial, an astonishing exercise of self-restraint, to write such a sentence as that which we have quoted. He did, however, leave himself a loophole of escape from the rigidity of his own rule; for he promised that "if the author has anything to suggest towards a change of text, not supported by any copies now extant, he will offer it separately in his Prolegomena."

The caution which Bentley expressed has been imitated by most of the great critics since his day, with the exceptions of Lachmann and Hort. But of the lesser men who have anticipated Hort in claiming to correct the text against all the MSS., it must be admitted that their success has been but slight, and that the praise which they have won has been largely, if not wholly, self-bestowed. Conservative critics like Scrivener would allow no such proceeding as conjectural emendation. "It is," says he, "now agreed among competent judges that *Conjectural Emendation* must never be resorted to, even in passages of acknowledged difficulty: the absence of proof that a reading proposed to be substituted for the common one is actually supported by some trustworthy document being of itself a fatal objection to our receiving it"; and again, "the reading to which no manuscript, or old version, or primitive Father has borne witness, however plausible and (for some purposes) convenient, cannot safely be accepted as genuine or even probable." But Scrivener leaves something like a loophole, for he goes on to say that "there may still remain a few passages respecting which we cannot help framing a shrewd suspicion that the original reading differed from any form in which they are now presented to us." That is, we may believe the text to be hopelessly wrong, but we must not venture, even by the simplest change, to put it right.

It need hardly be said that Dr. Burgon goes further than Dr. Scrivener: he attacks Dr. Hort's emendations fiercely and then says, " Some will be chiefly struck by the conceit and presumption of such suggestions as the foregoing. A yet larger number, as we believe, will be astonished by their essential foolishness.[1] For ourselves, what surprises us is the fatal misapprehension they evince of the true office of Textual Criticism as applied to the New Testament. *It never is to invent* new readings, but only to adjudicate between old and conflicting ones." And then, after setting Dr. Hort down for conceit, presumption and essential foolishness, he goes on to ask him " to consider whether he does not bring himself directly under the awful malediction with

[1] This is something like the language in which Conyers Middleton attacked Bentley's proposals: " So much vanity, pedantry, blunder and self-contradiction were hardly ever found together before within the compass of a single sheet."

which the beloved disciple concludes and seals up the Canon of Scripture."

But I was only incidentally referring to the possibility that the text may sometimes be wrong. Take such simple cases as the opening of the third epistle of John, where the Papyri show that the conventional opening for a letter is not περὶ πάντων but πρὸ πάντων; not "Concerning all things I pray," &c, but "First of all I hope you are well"; or such a case as I Cor. i. 13, where the negative μή has dropped before the repeated syllables of μεμέρισται. So that the ordinary translation "Is Christ divided?" is very nearly right. And so on in ever so many places.

What I want to do in this lecture is not to discuss and defend the general principle of conjectural emendation, but to consider the authorship of the Epistle to the Hebrews. As you are aware, there is a hypothesis before the world which was proposed by Dr. Harnack several years since, according to which the anonymous writing (call it epistle, or call it sermon, or address, or homily) is to be credited to the joint authorship of Aquila and Priscilla, the friends of Paul who are mentioned in the Acts and occasionally elsewhere in the New

Testament—with a distinct preference for Priscilla as the predominant partner (a preference which has some evidence in its favour from the order of the names in the text of the New Testament).

It would be too much to say that the new hypothesis holds the field, for there are some quarters in which it is regarded as a *jeu d'esprit*. On the other hand there were not a few (like Dr. Peake and Dr. Moulton) who saw at once that it was an entirely reasonable hypothesis and capable of strong support: and I have myself said as much in public on several occasions.

It is not necessary to review at present the traces which Dr. Harnack thought he had found of dual authorships, nor to argue at length whether the feminine feature in the authorship might not be responsible for the lack of the preface or title to the book, and for the hesitation, in certain quarters, as to its canonicity. We will restrict ourselves to one single chapter of the Epistle and ask what light this chapter throws on the question of authorship, and whether it definitely decides the question or leaves it still open. The chapter to which I refer is the eleventh, one of the most striking sections in the book, and almost capable of being dissected out as a separate Bible lesson or tract. My reasons for selecting this chapter are three; first it is a chapter in which Dr. Harnack detected feminine handiwork; second, I had myself suggested some features in it which seemed to reflect the joint experience of Aquila and Priscilla; and third, there have been urged from this chapter or in connexion with it, some very strong objections to the new hypothesis, the facing of which will, I believe, help us to the right understanding and ultimately to the true solution of the problem. First, then, we are to let Dr. Harnack speak on the chapter; then we are to say a few preliminary words ourselves, and lastly we are to try and meet objections.

1. In a note at the end of his article on the Authorship of Hebrews,[1] Harnack remarks that without laying too much stress on the observation, we ought not to neglect to notice that in the catalogue of Heroes of Faith in c. xi., women are three times mentioned: in two of these references (i.e. Sarah and Rahab) the allusion is very far fetched. The mention of Sarah with Abraham is an astonishment to the

[1] Preuschen's Zeitschrift. 1900 p. 40.

expositor, and still more the abrupt intrusion into the roll of heroes of the words "women received their dead raised to life again!" And it seems clear that a tendency is here betrayed of a desire to incorporate women also amongst the witnesses to faith, for which the Old Testament furnishes very imperfect material.

The point raised is apparently a small one, as it is only raised in a note; but it is a very important one and demands closer and further investigation. It certainly does astonish one to find Sarah claimed as a great believer, when the Old Testament lays such emphasis on her incredulity of the divine promises; and there are some other exegetical difficulties in the passage.

In the case of Rahab the difficulty might perhaps be evaded by the consideration that the question of Rahab's salvation was a problem in primitive soteriology: some holding with the author of Hebrews, that it was a case of salvation by faith; others with James, that it was a case of salvation by works; while the harmonizing of the two statements was made by Clement of Rome, who was certainly a careful student of the Epistle to the Hebrews.

But even if we could isolate the case of Rahab,

we should still be perplexed over the women with their resuscitated dead, who can only be the Shunamite and the Woman of Sarepta; and why, it may be asked, should these be credited with special faith for miracles done by the great prophets who in this connexion are not even mentioned.

So the suggestion of "feminization" in the Epistle remains, and the only question is whether it can be counterbalanced or rendered more striking. Does Hebrews xi. feminize? That is the question.

2. In my own reading of this chapter I was struck with the stress laid on the thought of exile by the writer, whether in recording instances from the past in which good men have had to leave all to follow God, or in inculcating the characteristic Christian grace of detachment, which results from a right estimate of things transitory and of things eternal.

And I have hazarded the conjecture that in most cases where the grace of detachment is in a high state of development, it is connected with outward forms of detachment, which have providentially been the stepping-stones into the higher experiences. Now we do not say that unworldliness and *Heimweh* are found only in the Epistle to the Hebrews, but they are found so emphatically there and especially in the eleventh chapter, that one is disposed to believe that it is an exile that writes and that enforced wanderings have laid the foundation for the doctrine and experience that "there remaineth a rest to the people of God." And just as Browning added as a corollary to this verse the words "And I have had trouble enough, for one," so we may consider the words to be not merely an addendum, but the very premiss of the argument.

Now when we read our chapter through, we find—

(1) That Abraham was one of Faith's exiles: that he went in search of a promised land; that Isaac and Jacob were also dwellers in tabernacles, and they all looked for a city of God at the end of or beyond the tent-life. All this patriarchal circle confessed that they were strangers and pilgrims in the earth. Their talk betrayed their country. They might have returned if they would; but they are pressing towards a better, a heavenly country. God thinks better of them because of their passion for the better land.

Surely this is exile's and pilgrim's talk, and not merely the observation deduced from a superficial reading of the Old Testament stories.

(2) And what about Joseph dying in Egypt, and giving instructions about the return of his bones to the home-land? And why did he talk of the exodus of the children of Israel? We are astonished, too, to find that it was an act of faith when Moses fled from Egypt, and the incident is coupled with an allusion to the wrath of the king. Is it surprising that this chapter should be credited to an actual exile, and in that case the forsaking of Egypt becomes parallel with a decree of Claudius Caesar that Jews in general, and two particular apostolical Jews among them, should depart from Rome? So we write against this chapter the words, "An exile speaks." That the motive for the discourse was not confined to the subject-matter of the chapter, viz. "the making and fortunes of the heroes of God," may be seen from the way the writer strikes the same note in the thirteenth chapter: "Let us go to Jesus outside the camp, and let us bear His reproach, for here we have no abiding city, but we are seeking the one to come."

So I have suggested that the chapter which we are discussing belongs not merely to the sentiment of Christian people generally, whom Peter admonishes to live like pilgrims and strangers and avoid the attractions of the world and the flesh, but that it has a particular force in being connected with the experience of Aquila and Priscilla. If this could be defended, the argument of Harnack for the dual authorship or for the dual authorship and feminization of the epistle would be re-inforced.

3. And this brings us to the third point, viz. that from this very chapter there will be brought forward the strongest objections to Harnack's hypothesis, and it is possible that some of them may be fatal. And these objections are of two kinds: first, that if it be true that the eleventh chapter is feminized, the feminization is insufficient, in view of the available material, and therefore must be held to be accidental: second, that the chapter can be grammatically proved to come from a masculine hand. These are the two directions in which we now propose to carry the investigation, and we will take them in order.

(1) It will be seen that at this point we are definitely contradicting Harnack's suggestion that

the Old Testament was ill supplied with women heroes. For it may be asked, Why do you neglect Deborah? And have you nothing to say about Esther? And why should Judith be forgotten? And again if Barak is mentioned and Deborah neglected, whereas the Old Testament definitely makes Deborah the central figure of the emancipation, and puts the Song of Victory into her mouth, then it would be just as fair to call the omission of Deborah a case of de-feminization as to call the intrusion of Sarah a case of feminization. And in the same connexion Jael finds no notice—the one that was blessed among women in the tent and was therefore taken by certain fathers to be a type of the blessed Virgin herself (as I think I remember Bishop Wordsworth once expounding). Surely if a Jewish or Judaeo-Christian prophetess were writing the record of her race in epitome, she would not have neglected the Charlotte Corday of that particular time of distress. Or, to go one step further, if prayer and faith go hand in hand, was there to be no mention of Hannah's prayers? Should Samuel be definitely mentioned, and his believing mother be ignored? Or if Rahab is worthy of commemoration on account of the escape of herself and her family from the sack of Jericho, her lack of virtue being no obstacle to the reception of grace, why should Susanna find no place, when her case was one both of faith and of virtue? Should Daniel be made mention of—for he is certainly intended in the words "stopped the mouths of lions"—Daniel, who "came to judgment" in the case of the wronged innocence of the Jewish lady, and no allusion be made to her conflicts, prayers and deliverance? And if these feminine features are all of them wanting, what becomes of the supposed feminization of the roll of heroes? Surely Harnack must be wrong in saying that the Old Testament is poor in heroines, and the conclusion must be that the eleventh of Hebrews is insufficiently rich in them.

Now, in order to examine how far this destructive argument has weight, I propose to approach the subject from two fresh points of view; first, by comparison with a similar roll of heroes elsewhere; second, by a more exact elucidation of the persons intended in the eleventh chapter. We begin, then, by asking for a similar composition. For it is agreed on all hands that this is the meaning of Hebrews XI. Its watchword is Faith, but its subject is the praises of the elders. It is true that the roll-call is prefaced by a statement that the worlds were made by the word of God and that it is by faith that we understand this. But then this is preceded by the statement that "Faith is the mark of the men of old time": so we see clearly that the allusion to creation only means that the writer is turning the pages of his Bible for instances of faith, and recognises in passing that even in Gen. i. 1 we find a place for faith, in the conviction that the Seen is the product of the Unseen. But this allusion is only there for the sake of literary completeness; it amounts to saying that we will search the Bible through for this thing, from Genesis to whatever was the last book in the writer's Old Testament. And as we are going to examine the roll-call in Hebrews by the side of another famous roll-call, it will be necessary to find out, if possible, just what the last book in the writer's Bible was. And I think it is not difficult to see that it must have been the fourth book of Maccabees. The fourth book of Maccabees is not much read nowadays, and its authorship is unknown: for a time it passed under the name of Josephus, but it can easily be seen that such an eloquent treatise, with such flashing rhetoric, and such an acquaintance with Stoic philosophy cannot have been the work of Josephus. Moreover, it must be earlier. It is concerned with the praises of the mother and her seven sons who withstood the frown of Antiochus the tyrant and despised his laws. It tells of the triumph of reason over passion, and it glows with the hope of an immortal life beyond the pains of death or the tortures of the tyrant. The early Christian Church took over the Maccabees and set them amongst its saints, where the Greek Church still commemorates them, and this book, the so-called Fourth of Maccabees, is the text book, as I suspect, of the primitive commemoration. When the writer of this book has described in detail the resistance which the Maccabee mother and her seven sons made to the ordinances and threats of Antiochus (the keynote of which resistance is the two words μέχρι θανάτου, "until death itself"), and when the death of the seven sons has been followed by the suicide of the mother, he says that it would have been well to put an inscription on their tomb for a national memorial, and to say—

"Here lie an aged man, and an aged

woman, and her seven sons through the violence of a tyrant, who sought to overthrow the Hebrew polity. But they avenged their race, by looking away to God, and by enduring tortures even unto death."

(εἰς Θεὸν ἀφορῶντες, καὶ μέχρι θανάτου τὰς βασάνους ὑπομείναντες.)

Now if we compare the closing passages of Hebrews XI. with the opening words of Hebrews XII. we shall find that all commentators agree that the bede-roll includes the Maccabees, and concludes with them; but it has not been so generally noticed that Hebrews XII. continues with the Maccabees, and imitates the language which is suggested for their memorial. Look at the expressions, "Let us run our race also, looking away to Jesus (ἀφορῶντες εἰς τὸν Ἰησοῦν), for ye have not yet resisted unto blood (οὔπω μέχρις αἵματος ἀντικατέστητε).

So we may say that the Bible of the writer of the Epistle to the Hebrews ran from Genesis to IV. Maccabees. But I must not dwell further on this point, but return to the other bede-roll with which I propose to compare that in the Epistle to the Hebrews.

In the Wisdom of Jesus the son of Sirach there

is, towards the end of the book,[1] a celebrated chapter, which is commonly read in English Colleges on the day appointed for the commemoration of benefactors. It is called the *Praise of Famous Men*, from its opening words, "Let us now praise famous men." In Greek its title is "The hymn (or praise) of the fathers." The writer, then, records in detail the praises of Enoch, Noah, Abraham,[2] Isaac and Jacob, Moses, Aaron, Phinehas, Joshua, Caleb, Samuel, David, Solomon, Elijah, Elisha, Hezekiah, Josiah, Jeremiah, Ezekiel, the twelve prophets, Zerubbabel, Nehemiah: and then after a few stray references to earlier worthies, the writer settles down to dilate on the merits and glory of the latest hero of all, Simon the Son of Onias.

Now if we review this list, I think we shall see that here also the writer is turning the pages of his Bible, at least mentally, when he writes; the reference to the twelve prophets probably shows that he is working from a book. So he is doing just the same as the writer to the Hebrews is doing. And the curious thing is that he never

[1] Cap. 44.
[2] Notice the language xliv. 20, ἐν πειρασμῷ εὑρέθη; and cf Hebrews xi. 17, πίστει Ἀβρααμ...πειραζόμενος.

mentions a woman at all in the whole of his story of Israel. This, then, is the way in which a man would write the historical summary; and the observation and the comparison with Hebrews, strongly confirms Harnack's suggestion that the latter writer has feminized. It is either a woman, or a man under the influence of a woman.

But, having made this comparison, and shown how it works in favour of the Priscilla hypothesis, we can go a step further; we can try and get some closer idea of what the Bible of the writer to the Hebrews was like, and so make some further identification of the persons whose praises are there, at least in epitome. We will identify some further characters in the cloud of witnesses. The cloud, in fact, very readily becomes crystalline, though I do not think the interpreters of the Epistle have adequately recognized this. When we read the chapter carefully we soon see that the roll of the saints changes into a roll of the virtues of the saints; the names of the heroes and heroines are dropped, and their deeds only are commemorated; but it is not difficult, speaking generally and recognizing that we are making a Biblical study, to identify the persons behind the actions. No one, for instance, has the slightest doubt that "stopped the mouths of lions" refers to Daniel, and "quenched the violence of fire" refers to the Three Children; and it would be a perverse exegesis, which should try to add any other figure to Daniel because the plural is used and we are told that "believers have stopped lions' mouths and quenched fire." So we know that Daniel was in the Bible which we are exploring for. In the same way any one who is acquainted with the apocryphal books that tell of the death of Isaiah and his rapture to heaven, or of the murder of Jeremiah by his compatriots, will have no doubt that Isaiah and Jeremiah were intended by the terms, "were stoned and were sawn asunder"; the legend of Isaiah's death at the hands of Manasseh and of Jeremiah's end must have been in the hands of the writer of the Epistle, who may very well have had the traditions in a written form; but it is sufficient if we say that the thought of Isaiah and Jeremiah in the Bible History called up their traditional deaths. So we are encouraged to seek for further identifications and we know the way to go to work. The presumption is that we are dealing with Biblical matter, and that a single person or group of persons (as in the case of the Three Children), underlies each clause; though we do not know that they are restricted to single clauses.[1] But in order to make our identifications correctly, we must observe that such identifications were matter of enquiry in the first century of our era, probably within twenty-five years of the production of the book.

If, for instance, we turn to the first Epistle of Clement of Rome, c. 17, we shall find him speaking as follows:

"Let us become imitators of those who went about in goatskins and sheepskins, preaching the coming of the Christ: I mean Elijah and Elisha and also Ezekiel; and besides them those men also that obtained a good report."

Here we see (i.) that Clement knows his Epistle to the Hebrews, (ii.) that he has been identifying the characters in the eleventh chapter. Of the acquaintance of Clement with Hebrews there cannot be a shadow of doubt: he quotes it so often, that some early writers suggested that he might be the author; and it is curious that he never says he is quoting, as he does when he quotes

[1] The Maccabees, for instance, appear to be diffusely treated.

Paul's first Epistle to the Corinthians. So either the authorship was unknown in Rome, or, as Harnack suggests, it was suppressed.

Clement goes on to say that "Abraham obtained an exceeding good report (ἐμαρτυρήθη μεγάλως) and was called the friend of God," in which we see him combining the language of Hebrews with that of the Epistle of James. There are other coincidences and assonances, besides his larger quotations, by which we can see how thoroughly Clement has assimilated the Epistle to the Hebrews. Now let us turn to the fifty-fifth chapter in which Clement is enumerating the sacrifices which have been made from time to time through love of others. After allusions to pagan illustrations of the virtue of self-sacrifice, he turns to the Scripture and remarks as follows:

"Many women being strengthened by the grace of God have performed many manly deeds. The blessed Judith, when the city was beleaguered, asked of the elders that she might be suffered to go forth into the camp of the aliens (ἀλλοφύλων). So she went forth and exposed herself to peril and went forth for love of country, and of her people which were beleaguered: and the Lord delivered Holofernes into the hand of a woman." Bearing in mind what we have already said about Clement's acquaintance with the eleventh chapter, and the identifications which he has made in it, let us throw into parallelism this passage of Clement with Hebrews xi. 34:

CLEMENT.	HEBREWS.
Many women were made strong by the grace of God;	Out of weakness were made strong:
($ἐνδυναμωθεῖσαι$)	($ἐδυναμώθησαν$)
performed many manly deeds;	waxed valiant in fight;
Judith went forth to the camp of the aliens	turned back camps of the aliens
($ἀλλοφύλων$)	($ἀλλοτρίων$)

It seems clear, then, that the persons, who out of weakness became strong are in Clement's judgment women in general and Judith in particular.[1] But this identification in which Clement passes from the general statement as to woman's weakness, to the particular triumphant

---

[1] As a matter of textual criticism this puts Clement in evidence for the reading $ἐνεδυναμώθησαν$, which the Editors commonly discard. What is supposed to be the later reading turns out to have by far the earliest attestation.

instance, requires that the word "women" in Hebrews xi. 35 should stand higher up, or that it should be repeated. The text must run "women out of weakness were made strong, waxed valiant in fight, overthrew camps of aliens." But at this point the objection will be made that if we are in this way resorting to the dangerous expedient of conjecturally restoring the text, we must go further; we must correct the masculine word for valiant (ἰσχυροί) into the feminine (ἰσχυραί). If we do, I think we shall miss the point of the writer, who wants to say that "weak women became strong (men) in fight" and uses the masculine deliberately. Clement sees this and therefore explains that "women, made strong by Divine Grace *performed manly deeds;*" he is explaining the masculine adjective. So, after all, our conjectural emendation, as far as we have gone, need not amount to more than the displacement or repetition of a single word. But perhaps the suggested use of the masculine adjective may be thought too rhetorical a device for the Epistle to the Hebrews. In that case we must emend.

But this is not all that we learn from Clement; not only has he identified Judith as the woman who overthrew the camp of the aliens, but he goes on with another illustration of feminine courage. "To no less peril did Esther also, *who was perfect in faith*, expose herself that she might deliver the twelve tribes of Israel, when they were on the point to perish. For through her fasting and her humiliation she entreated the all-seeing Master, the God of the Ages; and He, seeing the humility of her soul, delivered the people for whose sake she encountered the peril." The allusion to Esther, following on Judith, with the statement as to the perfection of her faith,[1] suggests that we are still in the region[2] of Hebrews

[1] Cf. Hebrews xi. 40, μαρτυρηθέντες διὰ τῆς πίστεως, ἵνα μὴ χωρὶς ἡμῶν τελειωθῶσιν.

[2] And this is also clear from the fact that Clement goes on to the early verses of Hebrews xii., and discusses the value of chastening with a reference to the same passage of Scripture as we find in Hebrews xii. 6. The sequence in Clement is as follows after the praises of Esther; c. 56 "Therefore let us also make intercession for them that are in any transgression, that forbearance and humility may be given them, to the end that they may yield not unto us, but unto the will of God. For so shall the compassionate remembrance of them with God and the saints be fruitful unto them and perfect. *Let us accept chastisement*, whereat no man ought to be vexed, dearly beloved. . . . For thus saith the holy word . . . 'whom the Lord loveth He chasteneth and scourgeth every son whom He receiveth,' &c."

XI. and raises the question as to whether Esther also must not be found in the roll of heroes. But it is not quite so easy to define Esther's position as it was Judith's. Perhaps "escaped the edge of the sword" may cover the case, but the description is very general and can hardly be relied upon with confidence.[1] It depends in part on the unknown order of the books of the Bible in the writer's collection. We do not know how the books were arranged or what was the order of chronology deduced from them. As I said above, we are sure that the history ends with Maccabees: over and above the reference to IV. Maccabees, we have the language of II. Maccabees imitated as in Hebrews xi. 38 ἐπὶ ἐρημίαις πλανώμενοι καὶ ὄρεσι καὶ σπηλαίοις καὶ ταῖς ὀπαῖς τῆς γῆς. ("wandering in deserts and mountains and in dens and caves of the earth") with which we may compare II. Maccabees x. 6 ἐν τοῖς ὄρεσιν καὶ ἐν τοῖς σπηλαίοις θηρίων τρόπον ἦσαν νεμόμενοι. ("they were living herded together like beasts in the mountains and in the caves").[2]

[1] We might perhaps compare Esther xiv. 13 "Think not that thou shalt escape."

[2] Cf. also Psalms of Solomon xvii. 19, ἐπλανῶντο ἐν ἐρήμοις σωθῆναι ψυχὰς αὐτῶν ἀπὸ κακοῦ.

And now we have said sufficient as to the structure of the Praises of the Famous, and the conclusion must be that there are Famous Women in the list as well as Famous Men. To Sarah and Rahab and the Widow of Sarepta we have added Judith and Esther. So there ought to be no hesitation in saying positively, what Harnack said doubtfully, that the eleventh chapter has feminized. And if this be correct, the case for the authorship of Priscilla is much strengthened, by the removal of some of the strongest objections. We are still somewhat surprised at not finding a definite reference to Deborah, but what we have found is positive evidence, which silence on certain points hardly affects any further.

(ii.) There remains one further, and perhaps fatal objection to be met, the masculine grammar of the chapter. The eleventh chapter, like the rest of Hebrews, has the transition to which Harnack alludes from "We" to "I." In xi. 2 we have "We understand that the worlds were framed by the word of God" (πίστει νοοῦμεν κτέ). But this is only the "we" of the community, and so has no bearing upon "dual" or "multiple" authorship. On the other hand we have in v. 32 the words "The time would fail *me* recounting," &c. and here we have not only the singular but the masculine singular,[1] (ἐκλείψει με γὰρ διηγούμενον). And this masculine participle is the real rock in the track, if we want to refer the Epistle to the Hebrews (or even the eleventh chapter) to Priscilla. There remains, however, the possibility that, as it is a case of variation of a single letter, the text may have undergone correction. In that case we should probably find the original reading lurking somewhere amongst the MSS., unrecognised or unrecorded. So far as I have been able to make investigation, I have not found any trace of the supposed missing reading. And until such traces can be found, it is only fair to say that the adverse evidence at this point to the Priscilla hypothesis is very strong: and it would not be proper to cure the text of its difficulty by a conjectural emendation unless the case were already finally settled by other considerations. So we may leave the matter in uncertainty, but with the hope that after all some light has been thrown upon the meaning of the text, and that, sooner or later, decisive

[1] As my colleague, Mr. Maynard, pointed out to me.

evidence as to authorship may be forthcoming. We need not make apologies because we are not able to settle finally all the points that come up before us for investigation. There is much that will always remain obscure in the history and the interpretation of an ancient literature; on the other hand there is also much that can be elucidated. The twentieth century has its disadvantages but it is not a bad time to live in, for the genuine explorer. And if our lectures can only be decorated by the title of side-lights, we may hope that they have the merit of being fairly clear of prejudice, and that in seeking after further light, we have not added anything either to the fog that bewilders or to the darkness that paralyses those who are engaged in the progressive interpretation of the Christian religion.

LECTURE VI.

Further Reflections on the Art of Conjectural Emendation.

WHEN we apply the test of time, following Dean Burgon's appeal through Pindar to the "remnant of the days," who are the clearest witnesses and the most impeccable judge and jury, and ask how it fares in such an appeal with the conjectural attempts to emend the text of the New Testament, we are obliged to admit that it goes very hard with the emendators. This does not, by any means foreclose the question and prove that emendation is improper in the New Testament, but it certainly suggests for it a narrower scope than has been in the view of those who practise the art. For example, I practise conjectural emendation freely, and often spoil the margins of my book with it; but if I allow time to elapse and then go over the ground again, there is usually a tiny "No" to be written against the correction, with perhaps a cross-reference to some passage which shows that the text was right as it stood. Certainly conjectural emendation will not be justified, if we do not first take pains to understand to the utmost and from every point of view the passage proposed for emendation. Many a correction is ruled out by suspending the judgment and increasing the attention. The text was right after all, we are obliged to say; it was we who were the sinners and not the scribes. No doubt it is a sense of the exceeding sinfulness of other scholars, and of our own occasional lapses from critical virtue, which has caused the art of conjecture to fall, in modern days, into much disfavour. And then there is, in the New Testament, a wealth of manuscript evidence which seems to negative the reference to such an apparently subjective court of appeal as the mind of a scholar when he is perched on the judgment seat. Mrs. Browning, you will remember, speaks in *Aurora Leigh*, of her heroine's father as having the scholar's regal way of sitting on thrones and judging Israel, and that his margins were decorated with such notes as " Corrupte citat: lege potius." Well, people do not like regal ways in Biblical criticism: and it is not surprising that we should be sent back again to the manuscripts, and to the study of their internal relations, as if they should say to us "To the law and to the manuscript testimony of the law; if they speak not according to this rule, there is no light in them." Or they might quote from Ben Jonson,[1] where one of his characters is challenged as to the authorship of certain bills which are fixed to the pillars in St. Paul's Cathedral, and replies: "Sir, if I should deny the manuscripts, I were worthy to be banished the middle aisle [of Paul's] for ever."

Now in Renaissance and Reformation times they practised emendation with more freedom than we do, and often with remarkable skill. The reason for this is evident; that race of scholars was familiar with MSS. to an extent that is almost incredible to us; many authors whom we have only seen in print, they had only seen in written form, or at best in the doubtful texts of first editions based upon single copies, or upon very scanty re-inforcements of single copies. Consequently they had the art of conjecture, especially I think in Latin, at their

[1] *Every man out of his humour*, iii. 1.

fingers' ends, and they could often tell you at a glance what an author must have written from the mere scrutiny of what the scribe had made him write. Dean Burgon vigorously denounced two things; (i.) the inexpertness of critics who had never handled a Codex, (ii.) the folly of those who resorted to conjecture for the decision of the text. But he did not reflect that if his critics had really been familiar with MSS. and their collation, they would almost for certain have brought back out of their studies the art of conjectural emendation. It is hard for me to believe that neither he nor his friend, Dr. Scrivener, had any conjectures up their sleeves, when my own raiment bulges out with them to a degree comparable to the robes of a pious Franciscan brother whom I once saw smuggling cigars at Jaffa. It must certainly have been the highest form of self-denial in them to refrain from mending a text which they would infallibly have attempted the cure of, if it had not been labelled Bible, and decorated with a *Noli me tangere*.

From such timidity the Reformers, at all events, were remarkably free: perhaps Beza is as good an instance as we can quote of the artist at work in this field. Some years since my

The Art of Conjectural Emendation. 181

friend, Dr. Blass, published a little book called *Philology of the Gospels*, in which he emended a passage in the Acts of the Apostles (vii. 9), where we come upon the account of the people who disputed with Stephen. The text says they came from the Synagogue which is called of the Libertines and of the Cyrenians, and from Cilicia and Asia. Dr. Blass felt there was something wrong with those Libertines, and with the popular explanation of them, and he accordingly corrected *Libystine* for *Libertine*, *Libystine* being one of the classical forms for what we call *Libyan*; and by this restoration he threw Libya and Cyrene together, as geographical neighbours (cf Acts ii. 10 "the parts of Libya about Cyrene"), and gave them a common synagogue in Jerusalem. This was very ingenious, and after he had made it, Blass remarked that "the conjecture has not really been made so far as I know; nevertheless it might have been made by a reflecting critic." Blass did not know that it had already been made by Beza as early as 1559 and abandoned in his N.T. of 1565 out of deference to the MSS. Here was the "reflecting critic" in possession of the field before him, and I had the pleasure (it is one that springs from the

" scholar's melancholy, which is emulation ") of pointing out to Dr. Blass that the proposed emendation was also under the ægis of Le Clerc and of Spanheim and of Gothofredus, that it was quoted by Mill with disfavour, by Wetstein and Bowyer with approbation, that it is in the New Testaments of Griesbach and Knapp, and has a paragraph devoted to it in Schleusner's Lexicon of the N.T. Nor did this exhaust the history of the matter. So that it appears that if, as so often happens, the history of a good conjecture has for its sequel the exclamation " Pereant qui ante nos nostra dixerunt," the curse may easily involve a historical massacre. The tracking out of Professor Blass' antecedents was a work of pure joy to me, and I have somewhere a letter which he wrote me in reply. But the reason why I quote the matter is not to disparage Blass, whose emendation stood all the firmer for the support which it derived from the antecedent history of criticism, but in order to point out an instance, which may be taken as typical; of the sagacity of the great Beza.[1]

There is another beautiful emendation which

[1] For a further discussion of the matter see Expositor, November, 1902, pp. 377—399.

Blass suggested to John xix. 29 which falls under similar condemnation or, if we prefer, has similar early attestation. Blass proposed to read instead of "they put a sponge filled with vinegar upon hyssop ὑσσώπῳ," "they put a sponge filled with vinegar upon a dagger ὕσσῳ," the rare word ὕσσος, which means a Gallic spear, having been misunderstood. A reference to Bowyer's *Conjectures* will show that the emendation had already been proposed by Camerarius. But I must not loiter over Blass and his anticipators: we have been in the same net ourselves from time to time.

There is, however, one direction in which these earlier scholars were limited; the MSS. which they knew were mostly written in the cursive character and were comparatively late in date; consequently the typical mistakes made by scribes of such MSS. furnish only a slight clue to what would happen in the copying of a MS. written in the uncial character, where mistakes in the letters are quite different from those that occur in cursive MSS., and where the continuous script introduces perils and pitfalls of its own. Every stage in the history of a book has errors which are peculiarly its own;

and it follows from this that whenever we ascend to a fresh level in the history of the transmission of the text, we open out a fresh prospect of conjectural correction of the text. I have the greatest admiration for that form of scholarship which makes good corrections possible: it has an ease of its own, and looks more like instinct than reason, but behind the simple and convincing suggestion there often lies, besides the resources of what we call learning, a long experience as reader, as copyist, and as editor, without which the step to the successful correction would never have been made.

Probably the greatest man that English scholarship ever produced in this regard was Bentley. I doubt if he ever had an adequate predecessor or follower in this country: the bow of Ulysses is hard for lesser men to bend and handle. But how he enjoyed handling it himself: how obvious was his delight in a successful restoration of a corrupt passage, and how more than obvious was his Red-Indian satisfaction when he scalped someone else who had unsuccessfully attacked the problem before him. Here is a pretty specimen of both his art and his manner. There was a certain contemporary of his named Barnes who issued what I suppose might be called the Cambridge Homer of that day. In the course of his work Barnes tried to correct an obscure scholion[1] in which there stood a sentence as follows: "When he introduced the Trojan captives, he asked them from which of the Trojans (ὑπὸ ὁποτέρου τῶν Τρώων) they had suffered more, and they said from Ulysses"; now as this was nonsense, for the Trojans did not suffer from the Trojans, nor was Ulysses one of them, Barnes proposed to correct it, so as to read, "from which of them the Trojans had suffered most," (ὑπὸ ὁποτέρου αὐτῶν οἱ Τρῶες,) whereupon Bentley handled him and the passage in the following breezy style: "I'll give him the true lection with altering half a letter; ὑπὸ ὁποτέρου τῶν Ἡρώων, '*from which of the two heroes they suffered most.*' This is clear and neat. But our Professor, besides his botching the words, has sullied even the sense; for the captives were not asked what all the Trojans, οἱ Τρῶες, thought, but what they themselves thought." Bentley not only carried a scalpel, but he supplemented it with a bludgeon. One would like to see what would have happened if Bentley had been able

[1] *Od,* xi. 546.

to apply his skill with unlimited freedom to the text of the New Testament, though I do not forget that mere classical learning is insufficient, on the linguistic and philological side, at all events, for the elucidation of that text. It is true that he modestly disclaimed in his prospectus any attempt to introduce conjectures into the text, and stated that he would reserve what he had to say for them to his Prolegomena. But I doubt whether, if the proposed edition had ever come off, he would have kept to his engagement: he would have been sure to put some stars or daggers or other disturbing features in the text, after the manner of Dr. Hort, to tell people that they would never be comfortable till they had deserted the text for the Prolegomena.[1] And Middleton, in criticising the famous Proposals, says that Bentley broke his rule even in the specimen sheets which he issued as prospectus, and deserted the MSS. for his own better judgment in certain not very important points. If that be so, the rule applies that he who is unfaithful in little is unfaithful also in much, or as

---

[1] I admit that this is not borne out by the Bentley MSS. preserved in Trinity College; but then these are not in their final form, and the actual Prolegomena were never written.

I put it in other words, those Prolegomena of Bentley would have been uncommonly interesting reading. Another reason why we should probably have had a feast of fat speculations in the book that never appeared is that Bentley was suffering from megalomania when he issued the famous proposals, and megalomania goes very well with an over-fondness for textual emendations, every one of which suggests that its author is wiser that all the rest of the scribes and rabbis. Bentley was quite sure that his New Testament was to be the last word on the question; he would consecrate it, in Thucydidean language, "as a $\kappa\epsilon\iota\mu\acute{\eta}\lambda\iota\text{ο}\nu$, a $\kappa\tau\hat{\eta}\mu\alpha$ $\dot{\epsilon}\varsigma$ $\dot{\alpha}\epsilon\acute{\iota}$, a *charter*, a *Magna Charta*, to the whole Christian Church; to last when all the ancient MSS, here quoted may be lost and extinguished." That is what I call megalomania in prospectus-writing. And it consists very well with an undue zeal in correction on one's own account, and an undue approbation of the same.[1]

---

[1] But perhaps the last part of the sentence may only mean that a good edition is the best form of fire insurance: for in his letter to the Archbishop of Canterbury he writes as follows:

" My Lord, if a casual fire should take either his Majesty's Library or the King's of France; all the world could not

What remains of Bentley's work in the shape of notes and collations was utilised by Ellis in 1862 for a volume entitled *Bentleii Critica Sacra*; in which we shall find not a few emendations both to the Greek Text and the Vulgate. One which evidently pleased him, and may possibly be right, was his suggestion that in the decrees of the Apostles at Jerusalem for the regulation of the new Churches we should read an injunction to abstain " from pollutions of idols and *swine's flesh* and things strangled and from blood," thus reducing the whole of the ordinance to taboos on food.

I am satisfied that Bentley's admirers expected that he would deal freely in conjectures. For Dr. Francis Hare who wrote a pamphlet in approbation of Bentley's *Remarks on the late*

do this (i.e. restore a complete text of the Nicene period). As I have therefore great impulse, and I hope not ἀθεεὶ to set about this work immediately, and leave it as a κειμήλιον to posterity, against Atheists and Infidels, etc."

But then a more satisfactory fire-insurance would have been the reproduction of the MSS. and not the extracts made from them by Bentley, a thing which he pleaded for in his famous Epistle to John Mill. And there is the same inflation of language about the value of the text which he was going to produce as we saw in the Proposals. He evidently considered himself an inspired person.

Discourse on Freethinking says plainly that " the present text [of the N. T.] wants the help of more MSS. than have yet been examined or the assistance of *critic* [i.e. criticism] to supply the want of them ": he says further that Bentley has " given us a small specimen of this in your happy conjectures upon three passages, which, as far as I can find by my own conversation and my friends, are universally liked by the men of learning, who would be very glad so great a master should turn his attention to the Scriptures." Some people would say that this was like inviting the wild-boar of the wood into the Paradise. One wonders what were the three trial passages which so moved the admiration of Dr. Francis Hare and his friends. It may be worth while to try and find them.

From the Prolegomena to Wetstein's N.T., p. 155, I find that he proposed to refer at the proper points to the emendations made by Bentley —both those which he had publicly brought forward in the famous tract which he wrote under the name of Phileleutherus Lipsiensis or in a sermon which he preached on II. Cor. ii. 16 and those which he had privately communicated to his friends of which Wetstein inserted more than twenty in the first edition of his Prolegomena. So we may be reasonably certain that Dr. Francis Hare was alluding to what he had read in Phileleutherns Lipsiensis.[1]

The emendations, then, to which we refer are (i.) The completion of the sentence in Acts vii. 59, "they stoned Stephen calling upon ——and saying, Lord Jesus, receive my spirit," where Bentley suggests either that "God" should be added, $\overline{\Theta N}$ having dropped after ἐπικαλούμενον or "Lord" as if $\overline{KN}$ had been absorbed in the following KAI. This at any rate is harmless enough, and if an emendation be necessary, is in the right direction. (ii.) The attempt to emend the decree of the Jerusalem Council in the three places where it occurs (Acts xv., 20; xv., 29; xxi., 25;) by reading χοιρείας for πορνείας.

(iii.) The third, as I suppose, is his proposal to correct *Euroclydon*, the tempestuous wind, in Acts xxvii. 14; and to read *Euraquilo* or something similar. But this is not exactly a conjecture, for it was already extant in the Alexandrian MS.

---

[1] Note in passing that Wetstein says of the Bentley emendations generally: "I am afraid they are not so certain as they are ingenious." That is the way in which scholars let one another down in the matter of emendations.

The Art of Conjectural Emendation. 191

and confirmed by the Vulgate; since Bentley's day the Vatican and Sinaitic MSS. have come to light with the same reading, and have justified his judgment.

Well, there is nothing very terrible in all this. On the contrary, if there should come confirmation of any suggested emendation from fresh scrutiny of the MSS. or versions, as in the case just mentioned, the emendator takes high rank, and the man is the equivalent of a very good MS. Perhaps we may sum up the merits of the case as regards Bentley in the language of A. A. Ellis (*Bentleii Critica Sacra*, p. xxii): "Opinions of course will vary as to the value that should be assigned to critical conjecture upon the Sacred Text. But no Greek Testament scholar can deny that it has its legitimate field who considers by how many degrees the oldest even of our Uncial Codices is removed from an autograph of the writers, and that an error once made by a copyist would be propagated through whole families of MSS. Of the merit of Bentley's conjectures every scholar can now judge for himself: in some instances he certainly was happy enough to anticipate the readings of Codex B. At any rate it will be known what changes in the text he did think probable: and future editors of the Greek Testament will be spared the pain of insulting his memory by ascribing to him conjectures which he never made."[1]

We may now consider a volume, to which I have already alluded, in which the learned printer, William Bowyer, collected from all the books he had studied and from all the scholars with whom he was acquainted, materials for what he entitled *Conjectures on the New Testament*. He published this in 1772, in his old age, at a time when palsy was on him and when calculus racked him: and in spite of the adverse criticisms passed upon its usefulness and its accuracy, it is really an interesting book. Much of it is concerned with punctuation and such like editorial refinements, as we should expect from a printer, and not with textual emendation properly so called: some parts, too, are almost dissertations on difficult passages, taken from the margins of Bowyer's own Greek Testament; but the greater part are genuine *corrigenda et emendanda*. His learned friends are indicated by letters of the alphabet, and no key for their

[1] The reference is to Alford and others on Acts xv. 20.

The Art of Conjectural Emendation. 193

identification is given in the book itself (at least in the first edition); but from other sources I have succeeded in identifying all of them but two, and they made a very good phalanx of contemporary scholarship. The British Museum catalogue gives a list of persons who contributed emendations to Bowyer, and names Bishop Barrington, Mr. Markland, Professor Schultz, Professor Michaelis, Dr. Owen, Dr. Woide, Dr. Gosset and Mr. Weston; two of these names, Schultz and Woide, have been erased with a pen. With these two exceptions, the names are taken from the second and third editions (posthumous) of Bowyer's book, brought out by his partner, and we may almost say his Boswell, J. Nichols. But this does not exactly cover the initials in Bowyer; we have to identify B, L, O, R, S, Z and *Anon.* Of these the commonest is R, which stands for Jeremiah Markland,[1] the commentator upon

---

[1] Markland's correspondence with Bowyer is published and in it we find the following:

July 30, 1770.

"In mine to you yesterday I expressed some unwillingness of having anything printed which is written in the margin of my Greek Testament; I had not thought of an obvious expedient which has occurred since, viz., that my name may be concealed (the chief thing I aimed at), and at the end of such note, if any be made use of,

Euripides. O, is Dr. Henry Owen; L, is Bishop Law (except in II.Tim. i. 18) where it is corrected in the second edition to Bishop Sherlock; B (in Hebrews x. 30) is Bowyer himself; and *Anon* is Mangey, the learned editor of Philo, who had made many successful corrections of that author. So far we identify by the help of the second edition, except S and Z; and the third edition doesn't, I think, throw any further light on them. So it is clear we are in very scholarly company. And the book, which is interesting in itself, is much more interesting when the names are filled in.

Bowyer himself is judicious in his treatment of the subject: he will not suggest that any emendation shall go into the text without confirmation from MSS. Confirmation from versions he does not consider sufficient; and although he thinks that many emendations are indubitable, he tells us cynically that "they are not wholly useless . . . . as they set in one view the ingenuity of the several writers' conjectures or enable the reader to judge of the futility of them." I wonder what Markland and Mangey would say

may be put the letter R." See also Nichols' *Anecdotes of Bowyer*, p. 431.

to that! But it would be a mistake to suppose that Bowyer always left the matter to the judgment of the reader. For instance in Matthew xvii. 3 a certain Dr. Bernard had expanded the text to read "His face did shine as the sun, and his garments became white as the light of the moon." He justified the expansion by the suggestion that the word for moon Σελήνη had been abbreviated by means of its first letter Σ, and that this letter had been lost or ignored because it repeated the last letter of the word for light (φῶς). Upon which Bowyer remarks, "A moon-shine emendation." At other times he explains why a conjecture is not to be admitted: thus when in Mark vi. 49 "Every one shall be salted with fire," Joseph Scaliger proposed to read πᾶσα πυρία, "every sacrifice of flour shall be salted," with reference to Lev. ii. 13, Bowyer remarks that "for the word πυρία no authority hath yet been found." And he continues in what must be meant for irony, "others read πυρά, 'every *funeral pyle* shall be salted,' a custom, for which, I believe we have as little authority." One begins to suspect that Bowyer was little short of being a scholar and somewhat in danger of being a wit.[1]

[1] He evidently enjoys telling a story of the pains his

The value, of course, of the Bowyer collection is precisely the value of the separate brains from which it has been made; and of these Markland is the ablest. His Greek Testament, or, as I rather suspect, his Annotated Copy of Bengel's *Gnomon*, was the mine from which Bowyer chiefly worked; and some of the Markland corrections are certainly felicitous. For example, in Acts xvii. 14 we are told that the brethren sent Paul away to go as if to the sea. Markland asks, "To *what* sea; in order to go *whither*? Perhaps Θεσσαλίαν, i.e. we are to read *Thessaly* for *Thalassa*, the sea. Beza's MS., in the next verse, after 'Ἀθηνῶν reads, παρῆλθε δὲ τὴν Θεσσαλίαν, ἐκωλύθη γὰρ εἰς αὐτοὺς κηρύξαι, &c. Whence could this writer say St. Paul was hindered from preaching in Thessaly, if Thessaly had not been mentioned before?" The force of this would have been even greater if the parallel passage in Acts xvi. 8 had been quoted: "they came over

late friend, Mr. Maittaire, had taken to make sense of a bit of impossible Greek from which a preposition had dropped in Bowyer's own printing office; he explains that such errors at the beginning of lines are common, and would ask his friend's pardon if ghosts know how to take an apology: "I should ask pardon of this Gentleman (scirent si agnoscere manes) for having been accessory to creating him all this unnecessary trouble."

The Art of Conjectural Emendation. 197

against *Mysia*, and essayed to go into Bithynia, but the spirit of Jesus suffered them not and they passed by *Mysia*." Whether, therefore, we accept the Bezan reading or not, the argument that Thessaly should have stood in the text is confirmed.

But we must not spend more time over Bowyer; his book is a store-house of information on the history of N.T. criticism, even if the conjectures themselves suffer the fate of being unappreciated by the succeeding days.

In our own time there has been a remarkable reassertion of the right of conjecture both in England and in Holland. I hope that here at home we are past the stage where the practice is considered illicit, and that we shall not be deterred from going some way with it, because the Dutch are considered to have gone too far in the same direction. Amongst those to whom attention may be drawn, we may select: Dr. Taylor, the late Master of St. John's College, Cambridge, and Dr. Hort.

Of Dr. Taylor's skill in emendation, always founded upon great and wide erudition, the best instances may perhaps be found in the region of Patristic literature: but there are some striking examples in the New Testament itself. Perhaps the best of these is the obscure text in Colossians ii. 18, where the erroneous worshipper or incipient heretic is denounced who practises a cult of angels ἃ ἑόρακεν ἐμβατεύειν. The language is rhetorical as well as obscure. What does Paul mean by in this connexion? Does he mean *invading* or merely *prying into* or *investigating*? Was the Authorised version right when it translated, with the assistance of a negative from the received text, "intruding into those things which he hath not seen": or the Revised version in rendering, "dwelling in the things which he hath seen," with a sense of hopeless perplexity reflected both in the weak word *dwelling* and in the marginal alternative, "taking his stand upon the things which he hath seen"? Here Dr. Taylor comes to our aid: the passage had already invited emendation at the hands of Alexander More, who was followed by Curcellaeus,[1] in the suggestion that we should read κενεμβατεύων for ἐμβατεύων, on the ground that a repeated syllable had been dropped. The restored word would mean that the person

[1] Curcellaeus in loc: quidam conjiciunt sic legendum hunc locum . . . ἃ μὴ ἑώρακε κενεμβατεύων.

The Art of Conjectural Emendation.   199

denounced was " walking on the air and talking the air ": we might perhaps render the passage, " talking windily of what he has seen." At this point, after a modification proposed by Lightfoot, Dr. Taylor proposed to read ἀέρα κενεμβατεύων, which gets rid of the repeated syllable, and differs only by a single letter from the MS. reading, a charming simplification: we might now translate " walking, as it were, on the wind." This passage is particularly profitable to study, because it shows how the problem passes from mind to mind, each scholar making some improvement on the suggestion of his predecessor, until at last a very simple and convincing solution is reached. You will like to know, however, what Dr. Burgon said about this, and he was almost bound to say something, after he had ordered all conjectural emendations and all conjectural emendators to the door. Here is his comment:

"The 'not' was sometimes accidentally omitted in some very ancient exemplar. This happens not unfrequently in codices of the type of ℵ and B. A famous instance occurs at Colossians ii. 18 (ἃ μὴ ἑώρακεν ἐμβατεύων, *prying into the things he hath not seen*);

where ℵ * A.B.D.* and a little handful of suspicious documents leave out the 'not.' Our Editors rather than recognise this blunder (so obvious and ordinary!) are for conjecturing ἃ ἑόρακεν ἐμβατεύων into ἀέρα κενεμβατεύων which (if it means anything at all) may as well mean, 'proceeding on an airy foundation to offer an empty conjecture.' "

That was very witty, but not very wise. For several very good hands helped in the making of the final conjecture in its varied stages from More to Taylor, and amongst the editors from Curcellaeus to Hort.

Of Dr. Hort's own skill in this direction, one can only say that, as far as it went, it was very high, and in some respects comparable to Bentley's. It was, however, skill within too narrow a circle: Dr. Hort was so sure that the text which he edited from the MSS. was in the closest approach to the original autographs, that he allowed himself no room to move in making conjectures. And on that account his emendations have a tendency to be either unduly microscopic or somewhat wooden. Yet I believe he really enjoyed a good emendation, whether made by himself or by others. My own intimate acquaintance with him

The Art of Conjectural Emendation. 201

began over an emendation in the text of Hermas on the name of a Jewish angel, which he at once seized upon to prove that Hermas had used the text of Daniel in the translation of Theodotion; and this led to a battle of giants in which I was a mere looker-on, (engaged like Rosalind in *As You Like It* with the desire to be invisible and "catch the strong fellow by the leg.") Alas! the problem started is still unsolved, in part; and of those that fought over it, Dr. Salmon and Dr. Hort are gone, and only Dr. Gwynn and myself remain, neither of whom expects to have the last word.

When I was editing, very imperfectly, some fragments of Philo which I had found, I remember Dr. Hort made one lovely emendation for me, by reference to a passage in Plato, but he would by no means allow his name to be attached to it. I ought, of course, to have explained that the correction came from a learned friend. I do acknowledge my fault this day, and pull off my peacock's feather.

One of the simplest and most interesting of Hort's conjectures is that which he made in a passage in II Maccabees (iv. 4). It has been incorporated in the Revised Version;

where we are informed on the margin that "The Greek as commonly read means *Apollonius* as being the *Governor of Coele-Syria and Phoenicia did rage and increase.*" For *did rage*, &c. μαίνεσθαι ἕως, Dr. Hort suggested the very simple correction Μενέσθεως, according to which the Revisers translate "Apollonius the Son of Menestheus, the Governor of Coele-Syria and Phoenicia, was increasing Simon's malice."

The only objection to this is that in iii. 5, Apollonius is called the son of Thraseas: so the Revisers have to announce on their margin that this is probably a corruption, or else they could not follow Hort in iv. 4. Thus one conjecture leads to another!

So much having been said with regard to English emendators, we ought not entirely to neglect the Continental scholars. The Dutch, in particular, have made this their special field, and one has only to recall the names of Cobet, of Bakhuyzen, of van Manen and Naber and Baljon, the brilliant Utrecht professor who was recently taken from us, to make it clear that in the field of conjectural criticism from the Dutch point of view, no small commodity of brains has been engaged. But it is interesting to note that even

The Art of Conjectural Emendation. 203

in Holland the emendators do not always agree: for instance Naber says of van Manen that "van Manen would have done better to have passed over a certain emendation in silence, but, that is van Manen's eternal fault: you would say that in his garden the tree of knowledge of good and evil was absolutely sterile."[1]

And in connexion with that severe and sarcastic judgment, it is interesting to note that Naber[2] is as sure of his own corrections as he is doubtful of those of others. He handles Acts xix. 16, for instance, where the seven sons of Sceva appear to reduce to two, because the evil spirit that they are trying to cast out overmasters them *both*, and declares that we must replace ἀμφοτέρων (both) by ἄφνω (suddenly). "Let us not doubt," he says, "for a single moment. I do not think there will be those who now contradict me." One does not see how it is so obvious that ἀμφοτέρων can be a corruption of ἄφνω!

Others of his emendations appear to me to be very wooden, as when he says that he cannot understand why in James v. 7 the husbandman

---

[1] *Mnemosyne*, 1881. p. 278.
[2] *Ibid*, p. 289.

should wait for the *precious* fruits of the earth. Why precious fruit? "Correct it," says Naber, "from τίμιον (*precious*) to ἔτειον (*annual*)."

Sometimes, however, Naber can be fascinatingly simple in the changes he proposes, and can do it, as Bentley would say, with the altering of half a letter. I noted one case in Acts xxvii. 38, where he proposes to read "we lightened the ship, by throwing with our own hands *the main-mast* overboard," reading ἱστόν (*mast*) for σῖτον (*wheat*). If we are to have emendations, that would seem the likeliest fashion in which to make them successfully.

In conclusion I have to apologise for certain attempts of my own to mend the text of the New Testament without the aid of MSS. Versions or Fathers: whether they are destined to be verified by subsequent discoveries, or to live by their own excellence without verification, is not for me to say. One form a modern scholar's ambition takes is that he may see his name at the bottom of a page with the words "Optime conjecit" against it. But then some one else must be responsible for the words.

One of my latest emendations was provoked by a reading of Luke xiv. 5, which has the en-

The Art of Conjectural Emendation. 205

dorsement of Westcott and Hort and of the English Revisers, according to which we are asked "What man of you whose *son* or ox shall fall into a pit, will he not straightway pull him out on the Sabbath?" The conjunction "son or ox" lands us in an intolerable bathos, whatever the MSS. and the Editors may say; and the MSS. are themselves in evidence for all sorts of attempts to get rid of the bathos, such as by reading "an ox or an ass," "a sheep or an ox." So one had to try and divine an initial reading in Luke from which all this menagerie of various animals and readings had started. Nor was this all. The problem was connected with that of the Synoptic Tradition, like so many textual problems in the Gospels, for Matthew had a similar saying (xii. 11) about a man who has one sheep which falls into a pit on the Sabbath. Either then the sheep is the original reading, in whole or in part; or it is on the way to it. Well, when we ask the question what is the objectionable animal for which all these varieties are substitutes (since certainly no one would have wanted to correct away an innocent original sheep) the only answer seems to be that the missing animal is a pig. And since the word for "son" in a MS. is commonly abbreviated by two letters Y C which exactly express "pig" (*hyios* being abbreviated as *hys*), we have at once the explanation of the reading "son or ox" and of the bathos resulting from it. Probably, then, the original reading was simply "pig." And when we restore this to the saying of Jesus which the Evangelists are trying to reproduce, we have the most beautiful case of irony in the New Testament. For it means that our Lord said in the first instance to the objecting Pharisees "Why, if even your pig (!) fell into a pit on the Sabbath, you would pull it out!" The picture of the Pharisee and his pig must have caught the fancy of the people, at all events they lived before the time when it had become impious to think of our Lord as humorous or ironical!

Perhaps the most useful of my own emendations, in the long run, will be those which are derived either directly or indirectly from the Book of Enoch. Every one, I suppose, knows by now that the Book of Enoch is a piece of pre-Christian Apocrypha, of which traces exist in the New Testament (in Jude, for example) although few realize how widespread those traces

The Art of Conjectural Emendation. 207

are. It was the discovery of the first part of the Book of Enoch in Greek in an Egyptian tomb that made the starting point for an important correction in I. Peter i. 12. Enoch tells us in his opening sentences that he saw a vision of the Holy One and that he understood the things which he heard in the vision, and he goes on, " I contemplated them not for the present generation but for one that was far distant." We recall at once what Peter says about prophets " to whom it was revealed that not unto themselves, but unto us, they did minister (διηκόνουν) the things which are now reported unto you." And this suggests that for " minister " we should read the word in Enoch *contemplate* (διενοοῦντο) so that the passage will now run οὐχ ἑαυτοῖς, ὑμῖν δὲ διενοοῦντο ἃ νῦν ἀνηγγέλη . . . and the correction is at once justified by what follows in the thirteenth verse, " Wherefore girding up the loins of your own contemplation (διανοίας), and being wide awake, hope for the grace that is brought to you in the revelation of Jesus Christ." Here the emendation was invited by the obscurity of the text, suggested by the parallel in Enoch and justified by the context. And it becomes clear that Peter was a student, and a close one, of the Book of Enoch. If this be established, the way is made very much easier for another correction which I had proposed to I Peter iii. 19: "By which also he went and preached to the Spirits in prison, which some time were disobedient, when once the long-suffering of God waited in the days of Noah, while the ark was a preparing." On this famous passage was built (to a large extent at all events) the doctrine of the descent of Christ into Hell, the disobedient sinners to whom He is sent being antediluvians and probably fallen angels. The quaintness of the doctrine is sufficiently obvious, and it is almost as incredible as it is quaint. It has all arisen out of a scribe's blunder in dropping some repeated letters; he should have read ἐν ᾧ καὶ Ἐνώχ, he actually transcribed ἐν ᾧ καὶ and left Enoch out; and then subsequent students, who did not realise that the Petrine formula ἐν ᾧ had nothing relative about it,[1] referred the whole series of statements about Enoch's descent into Tartarus to Christ, and on this perverse text and interpretation there has been built up a mass of superstition which starting from the Creed filled

[1] cf. 1 Peter iv. 4.

the mind of the middle ages with masses of legendary and apocryphal stories, and still corrupts the popular Christian imagination. In emending this passage I was, like my friend, Dr. Blass, endowed with antecedents. There was, without my having known it, a triad of previous conjectures on the part of scholars who had seen that the subject of the verbs had dropped and who had, by various suggestions, restored it either as *Noah* or as *Enoch*. As far as I have been able to trace the matter, the emendation is first heard of in Bowyer's collection, from a friend whose identity is covered by the initial S. This mask I have not been able to penetrate: but I hope I may regard him as a very acute and enlightened person, one of my own ancestors whose mantle I am quite pleased to wear.[1]

---

[1] It must not be forgotten that when the emendation is made in the text something has still to be done to restore continuity to the argument: and we shall have to admit that the text of Peter generally is in an unsatisfactory state, worse, I think, than most of the N.T. Epistles. It may be doubted whether it can be brought very near to its autograph, although something can be done to clear it. We find a curious blunder in 1 Peter ii. 8, where Peter is commenting on certain passages in which our Lord is spoken of as a stone of stumbling and rock of offence: he picks up word after word out of his prophetic testimony, as thus

It must not be supposed, however, that the whole history of the supposed descent into Hades turns on a single passage. There are too many descents into Hades in ancient folk-lore and mythology for this one to be altogether ignored or explained away. Whatever impetus may have been given to the Christian descent into Hell by the corruption of a single passage, the real impetus came from the side of popular fancy and imagination which would have made a *Descenus ad Inferos* out of nothing; the advantage of our correction lies in this, that a doctrine which once needed no Biblical support, because it was so congenial to the popular ideas of the world to come, is now supported by Church teaching and tradition which profess to go back to the Apostles and the Apostolic writings: and it is, therefore, very

"a *precious* stone and he that *believeth*, &c."   "to you that *believeth* He is *precious*."

(So the A.V. freely but correctly) and finally comes to the statement that "they stumble at the word, being disobedient; whereunto also they were appointed." But this misses the argument which is intended to carry one back to the opening of the prophetic passage, "Behold I set in Zion;" so we must not read "they were appointed," but "for which purpose he was set there" (ἐτέθη for ἐτέθησαν).

important to rectify that tradition and reconstruct our ideas of the next world. For, after all, the battle to be fought for purity of religion cannot be waged except as a conflict against superstition, which even at the present day, is so largely mistress of the minds of men. And it is only as we abandon, and persuade others to abandon, the untenable part of the traditions of the Church that we shall be able to preserve the Church itself, and shall once more convert the admiration and worship of mankind from the perversions of priestcraft to the simple and august and adorable Figure of Him from whom the Church derives its name.

LECTURE VII.

SIDE-LIGHTS FROM THE NEW TESTAMENT ON THE RELATION OF CHRISTIANITY TO THE GREEK WORLD.

WHEN we are searching for points of contact between the Christian religion and the older religions amongst which it emerged, the eminence on which we stand is commonly Mars' Hill, that rocky knoll at Athens where a wandering Jew once stood, with as was supposed, a commodity of new deities in place of old ones—an elevation from which one could physically look up to the Acropolis and its glories, and from which, if the Jew was right, one could spiritually look down on the Parthenon and all temples made with hands. Here the Old and the New meet, the Old somewhat faded, the New somewhat flushed; the Old anticipating the formula which the Roman Empire will some day apply to the intruding propagandists and saying "Non licet vos esse," "you are too young to have

Relation of Christianity to the Greek World. 213

a right to be: back with you and your new deities into non-existence!" and the New anticipating by prophecy the applied test of time that "that which grows old is on the verge of disappearance." And then, the short interview being over and the Jew released, he goes his way and they go theirs, and the sum total of it seems small; he has gained a convert or two, one man of mark, one woman without mark, and they have gained a day's dialogue and the excitement of an ephemeral debate; and the published report of the proceeding has a headline to the effect that there had been a dispute between a New Preacher and the representatives of the State religion, and that the New Preacher quoted good authors, and expects to leave to-morrow.

And then I suppose we re-inforce this result of the Athenian mission of St. Paul, by showing other places in his writings in which he betrays an acquaintance with Greek literature, and a possible University education with a Tarsus D.Litt. in the background, and finally conclude that there was one man, and probably not a second, through whom Christianity could have been carried to the Gentiles.

Now I have no wish to disparage or underestimate Paul or his mission, either at Athens or anywhere else; but we may safely say that he would himself have repudiated the idea that there was no point of contact between Hellenism and Christianity except at the single electrical discharge that was transmitted through his own personality. True, he was the great apostle of the Gentiles, but there were others beside him, and even before him. For the Jews were, in a certain sense, apostles of the Gentiles long before Paul was born: they were a missionary people and a successful missionary people in all the great cities of the world, and had encircled their synagogues by a *clientèle* of more or less closely attached converts. They had the real missionary art, to take as well as to give, to learn as well as to teach, and even in Alexandria where they opened their treasure house of Scriptures to the Greek world, they took back, in exchange, the knowledge of Homer and much of Plato and of the Greek dramatists. Some of them did so, half apologetically, pointing out that Plato had really stolen his ideas from Moses, and that, therefore, what was his was theirs by the law of prescription: and the more they proved Plato an intellectual thief and plagiarist, the more they showed that they were absorbing his teaching and its methods, and incorporating Greek ethics and philosophy with their own historical traditions and revelations. And it is just because the Jews were in such close contact with the intellect of the Greek world (and not merely with its trade) that Christian doctrine entered through a hundred doors to all the great cities around the Mediterranean. Yet if this be true, how strange it is that no Greek teacher is named in the New Testament (not even Philo, who was its nearest intellectual neighbour), that there is only a stray is only implied by the Epicureans, that Zeno is not hinted at, except through the Stoics, and the Divine Plato is not even mentioned. How are we to explain the silence? Was it intentional or unintentional? Why should Philo, who is almost a Christian, defer so constantly to Plato, and Paul who has almost ceased to be a Jew (for all his protestations to the contrary) barely mention philosophy, and then only to disparage it? Was Alexandria really so very far from Jerusalem as the Church History would suggest, instead of being, as Stevenson used to say of Samoa, the first house on the left after passing San Francisco—I mean Jaffa?

Paul tells us that the Greeks seek after wisdom, and that the said wisdom had no better name than foolishness with God. He must have been in the search himself to some extent, or how could he have known what the Greeks were after? One must follow the hounds, if only with one's eyes, to find out that they are fox-hunting: and it takes some reading to tell that a book or a system is rubbish. Is it wrong to speculate that perhaps Paul might have, in the studies of his earlier years, had an experience like that of Justin Martyr, to whom Plato held out the torch in the pathway of Divine Illumination, and who passed through the porch of the Academy as if it were the peristyle of a Christian Church and almost a part of the building itself? Was it perhaps from Plato that Paul learnt that the things which are seen are temporal, and the things which are unseen are eternal? But in that case why does he not mention his teacher? He is proud enough of Gamaliel, who perhaps led him nowhere except into Rabbinical subtleties and hair-splittings; can he make so much of a contemporary teacher, and so little, if he had known him, of one who held all the best men at his feet before Christ came, and a good many of the best men long after that event? Would Paul appeal to his Athenian audience concerning the witness of their own poets, and be absolutely silent if he found corroborations of his doctrine in certain of their own philosophers? To this last question we may perhaps return a partial answer: it is easier to recognise a quotation from a poet, because there is a change in the style of writing and therefore something which answers to quotation marks and invites attention; but when a philosopher is quoted there is no need of a formal introduction, because one is borrowing ideas, and not necessarily appropriating the language in which those ideas were expressed. Even in borrowing from Greek poets Paul is studiously anonymous; he leaves it to the erudition of Alexandria to identify his passages and say this is Aratus or that Menander or Epimenides. If he had been a pedant, he would have given you the author, the book and the verse!

But to return to our problem; we have suggested that there are many ways in which the first Christian thinkers, such as St. Paul, may have been in contact with Greek thought in its most noble systems: but we are still entirely in the region of hypothesis. We have not found as yet in the New Testament anything that may fairly be said to be interpenetrated with the spirit of Greek philosophy and traceable to its immediate influence. And it is quite open to any one to maintain that there was, at the beginning, no direct interchange between Greek and Christian thought, and that even the literary allusions of St. Paul to the Greek poets do not amount to much more than the conventional quotations which we put at the headlines of copy-books.

So let us first turn to the New Testament itself and look at it a little more carefully and closely. We are quite sure that it was not possible to go into the Greek world and ask "What think ye of Christ?" without sometimes meeting the counter-question "What think *ye* of Plato?" But whether they did think anything of Plato is a matter to be decided by direct investigation from the literature. And we may simplify the enquiry by the following considerations. Of the main body of early Christian teachers there are only two or three that come under review, as having special or extended knowledge. The average Christian man (whether Apostle or not), and then as now,

Relation of Christianity to the Greek World. 219

knew very little in regard to religion except what he had heard from his own Master or about him. He had one formula, "*Jesus said*," as our early collections of Logia show. He did not borrow that formula from the disciples of Pythagoras with their αὐτὸς ἔφα, it lay in the nature of the case. If he knew anything at all of Socrates, for example, it was comparable with what an average Baptist or Quaker knows of Buddha—the thinnest residuum of conversational tradition. Only in three directions does there seem a probability of special knowledge, in the cases of Paul, Luke and John: Paul, because he was well-educated and probably a University man; Luke, because he was a medical student and had to know Ionic Greek, and because he occasionally uses Homeric language; and John, because the Gospel shows a Logos-doctrine, and so does the Apocalypse, whether there be one John or more than one.

Suppose, then, we begin to test for average and popular knowledge about Plato. What did they have in their minds, these primitive Christians, when any one brought up the name of Plato? The answer is that (i.) they had a series of proverbial Platonic expressions which passed current in common speech and were understood by everybody; (ii.) they had, perhaps, heard that the visible world was connected with an ideal world, of which it was the outward stamp or expression; (iii.) they knew a little of the *Republic* which Plato had planned in the name of Socrates, and of the various social reforms which it involved. Now under these three heads, as we shall see, the early Christians expressed themselves, sometimes in approbation and sometimes in blame. We are able to get some idea of their acquaintance with and their mental attitude towards Platonic teaching, by watching what the early Christian fathers and the early Christian martyrs say on the various points involved. For example, it was matter of common knowledge that Plato had taught that the best government of a State would only be attained when "kings became philosophers and philosophers kings": here is one of the commonest proverbial saws from Plato. Accordingly when Justin addresses his *Apology* to Antoninus Pius, and to Marcus Aurelius and Lucius Verus and the Roman senate, he begins by observing that they pass under the name of "Pious" and "Philosopher," but that he means to find out whether they really are so. Rulers who are set to judge in a matter ought not to use violence or tyranny but to follow the leading of piety and philosophy. For one of the ancients has somewhere said that " Unless rulers and ruled philosophized, states can never be really happy." Of course Justin knew, as well as those whom he was addressing, that he was quoting Plato's Republic (v. 473); and he was leading up to the quotation from the very opening sentence: but it suited him to quote anonymously, and leave the quotation to produce its own effect. For he knew also that this was the great maxim of the Antonines, and that in their days Plato's rule was held to have been verified.

Now there is no trace of this favourite quotation in the New Testament—probably (i.) because the Christians were not immediately engaged in the reconstruction of civil society but in the amendment of their own lives and the lives of others; (ii.) because if they had been so engaged, they would not for a moment have exchanged their faith that the saints shall judge the world for a maxim that philosophers ought to be in high places. So we need not expect to find anything in the New Testament that illustrates Platonic doctrine on this matter.

The next bit of Platonic teaching which caught the Christian imagination, and in early times made them elevate Plato to the rank of a Divine prophet, was the study of Justice and Injustice in the *Republic*, and the way in which the Just man is overborne, victimized and destroyed by the successful unjust man. Glaucon has undertaken to prove to Socrates that the life of the unjust man is preferable to that of the just man; and in order to make the decision between the two characters quite certain, he proposes to perfect them for their assigned parts, the just man is to be made perfectly just, and the unjust man perfectly unjust. "Let us," he says, "make no deduction either from the injustice of the unjust or from the justice of the just, but let us suppose each to be perfect in his own line of conduct! And since the unjust man must not be found out, for that would prove him a mere bungler in his art, he must ever appear to be just when he is most unjust." And so Glaucon goes on elaborating his characters until at last Socrates interrupts with the remark "Heavens! my dear Glaucon, you are polishing them up as if they were a couple of statues." "I do my best," says Glaucon: and then he proceeds to tell Socrates what the end of it will be. He begs Socrates to forgive the coarseness of his description. He is really speaking for the eulogists of injustice, who will tell us that, " the just man will be scourged, racked, fettered, will have his eyes gouged out, and at last, after suffering every kind of torture, will be impaled (or crucified); and thus he will learn that it is best to resolve not to be just, but to seem to be so."[1]

It is not surprising that early Christian writers were impressed by this language, and regarded it as almost a prophecy of Jesus Christ's sufferings and death. Indeed Clement of Alexandria quotes the passage with the remark that Plato was only just short of being a prophet.[2] But then Clement was an omnivorous reader as well as a philosopher and was sure to quote the passage, and could hardly miss the prophetic suggestion, and he does actually quote it twice. No doubt many other Christians did the same. Perhaps we can get a fair idea of the impression which this great passage in the second book of the

[1] Plato *Rep.* ii. 362.
[2] Clem.-Alex: *Strom* v. 714.

Republic may have made on early Christian readers by observing how it has affected a great scholar of our own day. M. Salomon Reinach, who has been trying to prove that Jesus Christ was never really crucified, actually takes this passage, or at all events the popular opinions which it enshrines, as being the *fons et origo* of the Christian belief that Jesus Christ died upon the Cross. I will quote you his very words:[1]

"The idea of the Just man put to death on the Cross was certainly popular in antiquity. In fact Glaucon expresses himself as follows in the Republic [then comes the quotation]; so this is no invention of Plato; he is simply alluding to a popular story which testifies to the impotence of virtue before human villainy. This story, like so many others in Plato, may be of Orphic origin: the conclusion which results is the necessity of supra-terrestrial sanctions. We have here an evident proof that the story of the Crucified Just man was known long before the Passion."

We need not spend time in discussing M. Reinach's reduction of the Christian history to zero on the faith of a supposed Orphic prediction. I quote him simply to show that it

[1] *Cultes Mythes et Religions* iii. 21.

would not be strange if an early Christian reading his Plato or hearing it quoted or read, should have said that the passage in Plato was very like a prophecy of the Passion. I am not able, however, to produce any early instance to prove that the passage about the Crucified just man had made an impression in New Testament times.

But let us in the study of the passage quoted go back a little further to where the antithesis is being developed by Glaucon between the Just and the Unjust man. "We must," says he, "perfect them before we can rightly estimate their characters." Have you ever read in the New Testament anything like that? Will this be a free rendering of Glaucon's hypothesis?

"He that is unjust, let him do injustice still more: and he that is filthy, let him be made still more filthy; and he that is just, let him do justice yet more; and he that is holy, let him be made still more holy" (*Apoc.* xxii. 11).

Our Revisers, following too closely the Authorised Version, translated "He that is unrighteous, let him be unrighteous still," but they put on the margin the proper translation "yet more," which makes the parallel with Glaucon.

Here then is the key to the mysterious passage,

Revelation xxii. 11: it is an expansion of the Platonic suggestion, "good must be better and bad worse, and then we will judge." It occurs very abruptly in the Apocalypse, without any obvious connection fore or aft; it seems to be quoted as something which every one would understand; when we know where it comes from, perhaps we can see why the Judge stands at the doors in the next verse and why His reward is with Him.

Moreover we now begin to see daylight in a new direction. The closing chapters of the Revelation are the vision of the New Jerusalem, and the writer has shown by his quotation that he has the Republic of Plato in his mind when he is building his City. The ideal State of Hellenism and the ideal City of Christianity are now definitely brought into connexion. This is very important and will lead to some further interesting observations. The conception of a New Jerusalem, or of an upper Jerusalem is not to be derived, in the first instance, from any Greek attempt at State or City-structure. The doctrine of a New Jerusalem was the outcome naturally of the many Old Jerusalems which were destroyed, and it is always on a ruin that the

New City rises. But there are no ruins like those of the Jewish War under Vespasian and Titus, and from them the flight was perhaps finally taken from the actual to the ideal, from the Jerusalem below to Jerusalem above: it had indeed been taken before, for Paul has it in his Epistle to the Galatians, and we can find it elsewhere; but at the last it was the great disaster that made the great faith. When the early Christians began to write on the subject in detail, they drew on many sources, canonical and apocryphal; one amongst their number drew on the oracles of the Greeks.

We have now alluded to certain sayings and passages of the Republic which passed into popular use. Our next point is the theory of ideas generally, and here it is very difficult to say whether any given New Testament passages have been directly coloured by the Platonic doctrine or not. There was so much Platonism in the air, that it is difficult to say whether anything can be defined which should imply literary dependency. But if there was Platonism in the air, then we prove contact generally between Christianity and Hellenism without an appeal to special cases.

Our third point relates to certain Platonic opinions which must have been in the minds of any who talked on philosophical subjects at all, opinions which could not fail to provoke either opposition or approbation. And if we try to put ourselves in the position of the primitive Christians, I think we can realize what kind of doctrines they were likely to pass judgment upon. Or, if we prefer, let us ask ourselves what we consider objectionable features in the Platonic reconstruction of society, and what we think of them; for we may be reasonably certain that the early Christians thought the same. Three main points are the following:

(i.) The doctrine of Communism, especially in the matter of women and children.

(ii.) The right to tell lies conceded to governors and rulers.

(iii.) The relaxation of the laws of chastity in the case of persons past middle life.

On the first of these points Socrates says, in the opening of the eighth book of the Republic:

"We agree, Glaucon, upon these points— namely, that if the constitution of the state is to be carried to perfection, it must recognise a community of women, a community of children and of education in all its branches; and in like manner, a community of pursuits in war and in peace; and that its kings must be those who have shown the greatest ability in philosophy and the greatest aptitude for war."

Here we have the doctrine again of kings as philosophers, and a summary of a long discussion as to the marriage laws in the ideal community, and the Platonic doctrine of a community of wives and children. It was this doctrine that provoked the curiosity and interest of the young men who were listening to Socrates, and they held him fast and would not let him go until he had explained to them what were the methods under which the population of the new and ideal city was to be maintained and its excellence guaranteed. And this must always have been one most interesting feature in the development of the Republic: it remains so today: it can hardly fail to have been so in early times.

Let us hear then what a famous early Christian says on the point. Tertullian gives us the judgment of the Church in a single epigram: Omnia indiscretasunt apud nos, praeter uxores: We have everything in common, *except our wives*.

Communism at certain stages is almost a natural form of Christian expression. Christianity appears to have started from it, and in almost all subsequent religious revivals and reforms, it returns, more or less fitfully to its original programme. When the Christian religion declines, it drags its communistic ideas painfully behind it, as if it were not wholly able to disengage itself from them. For example, the Teaching of the Twelve Apostles, which is in many respects a down-grade book, continues the rule:

" Thou shalt not turn away the needy, but thou shalt share all things with thy brother, and shalt not say that they are thy own: for if ye are communists in things immortal, how much more in things that perish."

I consider it certain that Tertullian's epigram directs the sting in its tail at Plato and the Republic: and the emphasis in the sentence is on the last clause.[1] We may be sure that many an early Christian said the same thing, only perhaps not quite so succinctly. Here, then, is

---

[1] Tertullian: *Apol.* 39. It is amusing to observe that the Paris Tertullian of 1625, instead of recognizing the Platonic reference, employs the passage against the Anabaptists: "facit hic locus contra Anabaptistas."

one of the points of contact of the popular mind with the Republic of Plato.

The second point is the question of truthfulness in the ideal State. Should they speak every man truth with his neighbour and put away lying? It is one of the subjects that is most carefully dealt with by Plato. He examines the nature of the gods, and the nature of good men. Some of his sentences are noble:

"To lie and to be the victim of a lie, and without knowledge in the mind and concerning absolute realities, and in that quarter to harbour and possess the lie, is the last thing any man would consent to; for all men hold in special abhorrence an untruth in a place like that."[1] "God is a being of perfect simplicity and truth, both in deed and word, and neither changes in himself nor imposes upon others."[2]

But then after his noble defence of truth as characteristic both of God and the good man, he adopted the theory of the medicinal lie, to be kept in the hands of the guardians and physicians of the State, and out of the reach of unpro-

[1] *Rep.* ii. 382.
[2] *Rep.* ibid.

fessional men: and he sums the matter up as follows:

"To the rulers of the State, then, if to any, it belongs of right to use falsehood, to deceive either enemies or their own citizens, for the good of the State: and no one else may meddle with this privilege. Nay, for a private person to tell a lie to such magistrates, we shall maintain to be at least as great a mistake as for a patient to deceive his physician or a pupil his trainer, &c., &c."[1]

Lying, then, is a reserved art, practised by the guardians of the community upon the rank and file, presumably for their good. The rulers have reserved rights in untruthfulness.

Now it is quite certain that the Christian conscience as a whole is in revolt against the lying rulers whom Plato postulates. There are, of course, some exceptions. Origen for instance justifies the medicinal lie, but advises us to be very cautious in the use of it, for fear we should fall under the condemnation of Him who said, "I am the truth"! But then Origen is under the influence of Plato on this point and carried away by him. I do not think he was carried

[1] *Rep.* iii. 389.

very far. Christianity was not so corrupt in his days as to produce a Saint who should also be a Scientific Liar: and Plato himself must never be brought into comparison with Alphonso de Liguori, whose ethics, and the ethics of the Church which canonised him, Dr. Robertson Nicoll has so faithfully and so ruthlessly exposed in recent days.

The lying which Plato inculcated was not of the pitiful degraded kind which Liguori patronises and which Cardinal Newman was so hard put to it to defend. But whatever was covered by the Platonic doctrine, the Christian Church generally repudiated it, and I think we can now see that it is expressly repudiated in the Apocalyptic sketch of the New City. For if we take together the two points at which our conscience and the primitive Christian conscience revolt in Plato. the communistic marriage and the lie by authority, and remember our grounds for believing that the Apocalyptist had one eye on Plato when he wrote, we should see a new emphasis in the words (Apoc. xxi. 27):

" There shall in no wise enter into it anything that defileth, and he that makes pollution and lying (ὁ ποιῶν βδέλυγμα καὶ ψεῦδος). This is accentuated again in the judgment denounced upon "all liars" (xxi. 8) and upon "every one that loves and makes a lie" (xxii. 15).

And I conclude that in the vision of the New Jerusalem, the Apocalyptic writer definitely assails and contradicts the doctrine of the Republic of Plato on the points involved. He builds his City on the foundations of purity and truth.

There remains one final point to be discussed in this connexion, viz: the latitude in morals allowed to persons who are past the prime of life. It is a difficult matter to speak of, and requires a certain amount of paraphrase; but as it has an important bearing on the question before us and upon a particular passage in the New Testament, I may allude to it.

According to Plato, women were to be considered as in their prime, and in that sense serviceable to the re-inforcement of the community, up to the age of forty years and men up to the age of fifty-five. After that time the guardians relax their vigilance, "and as soon as the men and women are past the prescribed age, we shall allow them," says Plato, "free association," subject to certain necessary restrictions and with the approval of the priestess at Delphi. Moreover as the context shows, he held infanticide in reserve, in case infanticide should be necessary. It may well be imagined that such a social doctrine, weighted by such a practice, would provoke the deepest hostility on the part of the first Christian teachers. I am now going to show you that the protest against it is in the New Testament and that it can be read as directly addressed to the Platonists who held by the teaching of the *Republic*. I shall be obliged to paraphrase a little, but I will keep close to the sense of what I quote: it is in Ephesians iv. 17:

> "You are not to walk any more as the Gentiles do, with vain mind and darkened understanding and in alienation from the Divine Life . . . they gave themselves up, *after the prime of life was over*, (ἀπηλγηκότες)[1] to impiety in living shamelessly without restraint. *But you did not learn that from Christ*, you who heard him and were taught by Him, according to His law of truth, to put

---

[1] That, surely, must be the meaning of the passage: but is there any chance of emending the difficult word to ἀπηκμηκότες?

off the corrupt old nature and put on the new man, the just and the holy and the true. And further let us put away lying and be true to one another in our common life."

The passage is one that has perplexed translators and interpreters, and neither the Authorised nor the Revised Version shows any perception of the leading word in the sentence, which I have rendered by the paraphrase, "Being past the prime of life." Paul is not criticising Ephesian Christians for their moral laxity, but pointing out that they sit under another teacher than the one who gave lax laws to the Greeks, and that His teaching is purity and truth. The sentence, "Ye did not learn that of Christ," implies that the Gentiles, whom he denounces, had learnt it of some other teacher, and it can only be Plato of whom they had so learned. We notice, too, the connexion with the doctrine of truthfulness which we found in the passage in the Revelation.

I think it is fair to say, after so much of investigation, that both Paul and John antagonize the doctrine of Plato at its weakest points. From Luke I can find nothing bearing on the subject, but then Luke, although a scholar and perhaps a philosopher, has nothing to say of his own opinions, and we ought, therefore, not to be surprised that evidence, similar to what we detected in Paul and John, does not readily turn up. For Paul and John the influence seems to be clear. They read their Plato, or at all events they know the salient points of his teaching. Whether they had a closer knowledge than the popular knowledge involved in the points we have been considering, is the next thing to be investigated. We must come back to the study of the doctrine of Ideas, and of the Logos, who is the Idea of Ideas, to discover whether there is any definite overlapping of Christianity and Platonism.

We may, I think, be quite sure that the condemnations involved in the passages we have been studying, do not commit either Paul or John to an anti-Platonic attitude. There was too much that was great and high in Plato's teaching for it to be possibly disowned, except in offensive details. If it be true that the Christian doctrine of immortality owes much to Plato (and some say that Christianity went wrong in following Plato too closely in this direction) we can hardly suppose that the Church disowned or denied the teacher whose influence has been so profound. And we are perfectly free to examine for traces of Platonic teaching, without any preliminary suggestion that the earliest Christian teachers antagonised Plato from the outset. They opposed him, indeed, but it was at the points where he had to be opposed. But the affection of Justin Martyr for Plato is a sufficient illustration of what a hold the Greek teacher could have on the Christian saint. There is not the least reason to suppose that Justin had any affection for the ethical aberrations of the Republic: but Plato was greater than his mistakes: he was, for Justin and for many another, a Christian born before due time: he and Socrates and all their kith and kin who believed in the Logos and walked by his teaching, were reckoned to belong to the great company of the good and wise whom Christ fathers.

In what has preceded, our attention has been fixed on minute points and coincidences of thought and expression rather than on the general question of the agreement in philosophical conceptions or in psychology between Plato and the New Testament writers. The question of the doctrine of the Logos is something very different from the microscopy in which we have been indulging. Here we have the human mind in its highest flights, and we cannot avoid the discussion of the action and interaction between Greek philosophy and Christian thought. When the fourth Gospel makes its prologue with "In the beginning was the Logos," we are obliged to ask where the writer found the Logos. Did he evolve the idea himself and make the term to express the idea: or did he take it from Plato: and if from Plato, did he derive it immediately or may there be a connecting link or links, due to other teachers who have been engaged in similar speculations? Now these questions are not new, nor have they, as yet, been finally answered. If in these magnificent words Christianity became a philosophy, and if in the connected statement about the Logos becoming flesh, it became in the highest sense a theology, we are obliged to an enquiry how far outside materials have been used in the philosophic or the theologic structure. In an interesting article in the *Bibliotheca Sacra* for January, 1908, Professor Baljon, of Utrecht, gave the results of his enquiry into the indebtedness of Christianity to other religious systems. As I have said, the study is an interesting one, both in itself, and on account of the range it covers in the possible relation of Christianity to Buddhism, Mithraism or Hellenism: but the article has also a pathetic interest in being the last piece of work that dropped from his pen. Let us extract a few sentences from Prof. Baljon on the doctrine of the Logos. "Here" says he, "we have the known doctrine of the Logos, developed in the prologue of the Fourth Gospel, and which I take to be the subject of the entire Gospel. The theme is summarized in the well-known verse 'And the Word became flesh and dwelt among us.' This Logos doctrine is derived from the Logos doctrine of Philo, the well-known Hellenist. Although this philosopher was a Jew, his speculation is not immediately derived from the Old Testament, since, in its entirety, the Old Testament contains . . . no formulated philosophy. Here Philo built upon foundations that were laid by Plato. . . . The revelation of God is the Logos, the embodiment of the thoughts of God. God, in so far as He reveals Himself, is called Logos. The Logos, however, in so far as he reveals God, is called God. . . . In several points, such as in its well-known antithesis between flesh and spirit,

Relation of Christianity to the Greek World. 241

light and darkness, being from above and from beneath, the Fourth Gospel joins itself to Alexandrian Hellenism, &c."

This seems a very fair and moderate statement of the most pronounced piece of Platonism in the New Testament; but it must be confessed that there are many missing links before we can state a complete argument.

Now if we are right in the assertion that John derives his Platonic doctrine through a Philonic medium, it will be interesting to compare his attitude of mind with that of his assumed teacher. When Philo writes, he has one eye on Plato and the other on Moses. He is interpreting the one teacher by the other, with a view to an inviolable agreement between them. In the end, Philo will have held his brief for Moses, as the philosophic ancestor of Plato, so adroitly and so systematically that we shall have to say "Either Plato is Philonizing or Philo is Platonizing," so close will be the underlying agreement. Now the difference between the attitude of the Christian teacher and that of the great Jewish teacher is that the former is moving away from Moses, and taking Plato *en route*, while the latter is holding fast to Moses, and drawing Plato into his own position.

We may illustrate this by an observation which I recently made when I was looking at the text of the Book of Deuteronomy in one of these recently found Detroit manuscripts. There, before my eyes, were the opening sentences:

"These are the words which Moses spake to the people in the wilderness,"

and on looking at them I was at once struck by their parallelism with the opening sentences of the recently found Sayings of Jesus:

"These are the words (the wonderful words) which Jesus the living One spake, &c."

It was natural to suggest that the Christian writer had imitated the opening of Deuteronomy. In that case, there was an intention: we were being called from the words of Moses to the words of Christ. The very name of Deuteronomy to a Jew is taken from its opening Hebrew words; *Elle Debarim* is what they call it, or "These be the words": and it follows that every Jew would catch the meaning of the form in which the Book of Sayings was cast. They are an intimation that we are leaving Moses for Christ. Now turn to the Fourth Gospel. Here again we have something of the same kind. Every one sees that the opening is similar to that of Genesis. Is this a mere literary device, or is there an intention in it? Is the author replacing the Pentateuch, and displacing Moses, or only imitating him? If it had been Philo who was writing, we should have at once said, the author is keeping as close to Moses as possible: there is no antithesis: he corresponds rather than contradicts. But when we examine the Fourth Gospel the context tells us what was in his mind who wrote it: for we see a little lower down the words,

"The Law was given by Moses:

Grace and Truth came by Jesus Christ."

So there can be no doubt that, like the writer of the Book of Sayings, he is moving away from Moses, and that he intends to leave him presently far behind. And in imitating the language of the "Law given by Moses," he intimates that we are no longer under that Law but under the Grace of Christ. Thus the literary structure of the Fourth Gospel is like the literary structure of the Book of Sayings; they both answer to the Voice that came from heaven and said "This is My beloved Son, hear Him."

www.ingramcontent.com/pod-product-compliance
Lightning Source LLC
Chambersburg PA
CBHW060600230426
43670CB00011B/1904